THE
HEALTHY
COOK
100
WHOLESOME RECIPES
FOR BUSY COOKS

THE
HEALTHY
COOK
100
WHOLESOME RECIPES
FOR BUSY COOKS

ANAYA PUBLISHERS LTD
LONDON

First published in Great Britain in 1994 by
ANAYA PUBLISHERS LTD.
Strode House 44-50 Osnaburgh Street, London NW1 3ND

Copyright © Anaya Publishers Ltd. 1994

Recipes by MARY CADOGAN, JACQUELINE CLARK,
CAROLE HANDSLIP and LYN RUTHERFORD
Photography by JAMES MURPHY, ALAN NEWNHAM and CLIVE STREETER
Jacket design by EDWIN BELCHAMBER
Designer PEDRO PRÁ-LOPEZ
Food Stylists MARY CADOGAN, JACQUELINE CLARK, CAROLE HANDSLIP, MEG JANSZ,
ANNIE NICHOLS and LYN RUTHERFORD
Photographic Stylist SUE RUSSELL
Background Artist ANNABEL PLAYFAIR
Introduction by FELICITY JACKSON

British Library Cataloguing in Publication Data
Healthy Cook: 100 Wholesome Recipes for Busy Cooks
641.5

ISBN 1-85470-219-X

Typeset in Great Britain by SX Composing Ltd.,
Rayleigh, Essex
Colour reproduction by J. Film Process, Bangkok
Printed and bound in Portugal by Printer Portuguesa Lda.

NOTES

Ingredients are listed in metric and imperial measures.
Use either set of quantities but not a mixture of both.

All spoon measures are level:
1 tablespoon = one 15 ml spoon
1 teaspoon = one 5 ml spoon.

Use fresh herbs and freshly ground black pepper unless otherwise stated.

Use standard size 3 eggs unless otherwise suggested.

CONTENTS

INTRODUCTION

More and more people are beginning to realise the importance of eating sensibly in order to give themselves the best chance of enjoying a fit and healthy life.

Healthy eating means eating less fat – in particular the saturated kind found in meat and dairy products, less sugar, less salt and more fruit and vegetables, more whole grain bread and cereals to provide dietary fibre, more fish, and lean red meat and poultry rather than fatty meat.

This book is full of imaginative ideas for busy people who enjoy healthy eating but simply don't have the time to spend hours shopping and preparing food. All the delicious dishes can be made quickly and easily without any need for long lists of unusual ingredients and complicated cooking methods.

Discover how to make the most of the enormous range of time-saving cuts of meat sold in supermarkets nowadays: cubed meat for kebabs, thinly cut strips for stir frying, boneless pork chops and port tenderloin, plus a wide choice of chicken pieces.

Grilling and stir frying are two of the quickest and healthiest cooking methods. Stir frying is particularly versatile: meat, fish and vegetables can all be cooked this way (see Stir Fried Beef with Noodles, Stir Fried Fish with Tomato & Herbs and Five Spiced Chinese Leaf). The secret of the technique lies in cutting the food into uniformly-sized pieces and then cooking them very quickly over high heat in the minimum amount of oil.

When grilling lean meat or fish, always preheat the grill before using it; this way the high temperature sears the surface of the food, sealing in all the juices before you cook the food.

Store cupboard standbys such as batter and pizza base mixes, ready-made short-crust and puff pastry and canned tomatoes are all great time savers and can be combined with fresh ingredients to provide mouthwatering dishes in a matter of minutes.

Pasta – either freshly made at home or shop-bought – is perfect for the busy cook. Recipes such as Tagliatelle with Prawns & Mushrooms and Rigatoni with Pepper & Garlic Sauce can be prepared in the time it takes to boil the water and cook the pasta.

Fresh vegetables and fruit play an important part in a healthy diet, providing essential fibre as well as vitamins and other nutrients. The varied selection of vegetable dishes in this book includes everything from soups, starters and salads to main courses and accompaniments.

Fruit can be combined with yogurt to make a choice of delicious low-fat desserts like Raspberry Yogurt Ice and Light Chocolate and Pear Desserts, or it can simply be served on its own on a bed of crushed ice (see Iced Exotic Fruits).

Whether you are looking for a quick snack, a family meal or a light supper dish to share with friends, you will find a wide choice of healthy recipes to fit in with the amount of time you have.

CARROT ROULADE

SERVES 6

125 g (4 oz) butter
750 g (1½ lb) carrots, finely grated
6 eggs, separated
salt and pepper to taste

FILLING
6 hard-boiled eggs, chopped
300 ml (½ pint) mayonnaise
2 tablespoons chopped chives

TO GARNISH
salad leaves

1 Preheat oven to 200°C (400°F/Gas 6).

2 Line a 34×27 cm (13½×10½ inch) Swiss roll tin with foil; brush lightly with oil.

3 Melt the butter in a pan, add the grated carrots and cook gently until soft. Transfer to a bowl and beat in the egg yolks and seasoning.

4 Whisk the egg whites until soft peaks form, then fold into the carrot mixture.

5 Spread evenly in the prepared tin and bake for 10 minutes, or until golden and springy to the touch. Cover with a clean damp cloth.

6 Mix together the ingredients for the filling and add seasoning to taste.

7 Remove cloth and turn the roulade out on to a sheet of non-stick paper. Spread with the filling, leaving a 1 cm (½ inch) border all round. Carefully roll up from a short side, using the paper to help. Trim the ends and cut the roulade into slices.

8 Serve garnished with salad leaves.

LEEK & PEPPER SLICE

SERVES 6

875 g (1¾ lb) small leeks, trimmed
400 g (14 oz) can pimientos, drained

VINAIGRETTE
2 tablespoons olive oil
1 tablespoon hazelnut oil
1 tablespoon white wine vinegar
salt and pepper to taste
1 tablespoon chopped mixed herbs, eg parsley,
  chives, tarragon

TO GARNISH
chopped parsley

1 Cook the leeks in boiling salted water until tender, about 10 minutes. Drain and immerse in cold water for 5 minutes; drain and dry thoroughly, squeezing to remove excess water. Dry the pimientos on kitchen paper and cut into thick strips.

2 Line a 1.2 litre (2 pint) terrine with foil, leaving an overlap at the edges.

3 Line the base of the terrine with a third of the leeks, packing them tightly. Cover with half of the pimiento strips. Continue these layers, finishing with leeks.

4 Fold the foil over the surface and weight down. (A small board with 2 or 3 food cans on top works well.) Chill overnight.

5 For the vinaigrette, whisk together the oils, vinegar, seasoning and herbs.

6 Carefully unmould the terrine and cut into slices. Serve drizzled with vinaigrette and sprinkled with chopped parsley.

ABOVE: CARROT ROULADE *BELOW*: LEEK & PEPPER SLICE

WATERCRESS & LIME SOUP

SERVES 6

This soup is equally delicious served hot or cold. Don't overcook the watercress, or it will lose its colour.

---

50 g (2 oz) butter
250 g (8 oz) potato, diced
250 g (8 oz) leek, chopped
3 bunches watercress, stalks removed
1 litre (1¾ pints) chicken stock
salt and pepper to taste
grated rind and juice of 1 lime
4 tablespoons cream
watercress sprigs to garnish

1 Melt the butter in a large pan. Add the potato and leek, and cook gently for about 10 minutes until soft.

2 Meanwhile finely chop the watercress. Add the chicken stock to the pan, bring to the boil and add a pinch of salt. Add the watercress and simmer for 8 minutes.

3 Transfer to a food processor or blender and purée until smooth.

4 Return the soup to the pan. Add the lime rind and juice, check the seasoning and heat through.

5 Transfer to individual soup plates, swirl in the cream and serve garnished with watercress.

THAI-STYLE HOT & SOUR SOUP

SERVES 6

This soup uses typical Thai ingredients – dried lemon grass and straw mushrooms – available from larger supermarkets. Use button mushrooms, if you prefer.

1.5 litres (2½ pints) chicken stock
2 tablespoons dried lemon grass
1 tablespoon grated lime rind
salt to taste
3 tablespoons lime juice
¼ teaspoon chilli paste
¼ teaspoon sugar
½ × 425 g (15 oz) can straw mushrooms, drained
125 g (4 oz) beansprouts
1 bunch spring onions, thinly sliced
250 g (8 oz) frozen prawns, defrosted
2 small red chillies, seeded and thinly sliced
3 tablespoons coriander leaves

1 Put the stock, lemon grass and lime rind in a large pan. Bring to the boil, lower the heat and simmer gently for 15 minutes.

2 Strain the stock and return to the pan. Season with salt, then add the lime juice, chilli paste and sugar. Stir well.

3 Add the mushrooms, beansprouts and spring onions. Simmer for 1 minute.

4 Add the prawns and simmer for a few seconds to heat through.

5 Serve in individual bowls, sprinkled with chilli slices and coriander leaves.

MUSHROOM RAGOÛT

SERVES 4

Find as many different types of mushrooms as you can to make this ragoût as flavoursome as possible.

50 g (2 oz) butter
2 shallots, finely chopped
500 g (1 lb) mixed mushrooms, eg shitake, oyster,
    chanterelles
4 tomatoes, peeled, seeded and diced
1 tablespoon chopped chives
salt and pepper to taste
2 tablespoons crème fraîche

TO SERVE
snipped chives
croûtes (fried bread) or toast

1 Melt the butter in a pan, add the shallots and cook until softened.

2 Add the mushrooms and cook, covered, for 5 minutes until softened and beginning to release liquid.

3 Stir in the tomatoes and chives. Simmer for a few seconds, until thickened. Season and stir in the crème fraîche.

4 Serve immediately, sprinkled with chives and accompanied by the croûtes or toast.

TOMATO SOUFFLÉS

SERVES 6

6 firm beef tomatoes
25 g (1 oz) butter
1 tablespoon tomato purée
1 teaspoon sugar
1 spring onion, finely chopped
salt and pepper to taste
15 g (½ oz) flour
125 ml (4 fl oz) hot milk
1 tablespoon freshly grated Parmesan cheese
2 eggs, separated
basil leaves to garnish

1 Preheat oven to 180°C (350°F/Gas 4).

2 Slice the top third off the tomatoes and discard. Using a teaspoon, scoop out the flesh, juice and seeds, reserving the flesh from 4 tomatoes. Leave tomatoes upside down on kitchen paper to drain.

3 Melt half the butter in a pan and add the reserved tomato flesh. Cook for 10-15 minutes until thickened. Add the tomato purée, sugar, spring onion and seasoning. Simmer for 2 minutes.

4 Melt remaining butter in another pan, stir in the flour and cook for 1 minute. Add the hot milk and cook, stirring, until very thick. Add to the tomato mixture with the Parmesan. Beat in the egg yolks.

5 Whisk the egg whites until soft peaks form and fold into the mixture.

6 Place the tomatoes on a baking sheet and fill with the soufflé mixture. Bake for 10-15 minutes until puffed and golden. Serve immediately, garnished with basil leaves.

SPINACH & HAM CRÊPES

SERVES 4

Cooked pancakes freeze very successfully, and can be filled with a variety of savoury mixtures. Try adding chopped fresh herbs to the batter, before cooking.

130 g (4½ oz) packet batter mix
2 eggs
125 g (4 oz) butter
250 g (8 oz) ricotta cheese
salt and pepper to taste
grated nutmeg to taste
500 g (1 lb) frozen chopped spinach, defrosted
4 tablespoons freshly grated Parmesan cheese
8 large thin slices ham

TO SERVE
225 ml (8 fl oz) passata
parsley sprigs to garnish

1 Preheat oven to 230°C (450°F/Gas 8).

2 Make up the batter according to the packet instructions (see note). Beat in the eggs to yield a smooth batter.

3 Melt a knob of butter in a small frying pan. When sizzling, pour in enough batter to thinly coat the base of the pan, tilting the pan to spread the batter evenly. Cook for 1 minute, then using a palette knife, turn the crêpe over. Cook the underside until lightly browned. Repeat this process until you have 8 crêpes, layering them between pieces of greaseproof paper as they are cooked, to prevent them sticking.

4 In a bowl, mix together 25 g (1 oz) of the butter, the ricotta cheese, salt, pepper, and nutmeg. Squeeze the spinach to remove as much moisture as possible, then add to the mixture. Stir in half of the Parmesan cheese.

5 Lay a slice of ham on each crêpe, then spread with the spinach mixture to within 1 cm (½ inch) of the edges. Roll up the crêpes and cut each one in half.

6 Layer the crêpes in a buttered ovenproof dish, and sprinkle with the remaining Parmesan. Dot with the remaining butter.

7 Bake for 20 minutes until golden brown. Meanwhile, season the passata with salt and pepper and heat through in a small pan.

8 Serve the spinach and ham crêpes garnished with sprigs of parsley and accompanied by the seasoned passata.

NOTE:
If you prefer, make up your own quick crêpe batter in a blender or food processor. Simply process 150 g (5 oz) plain flour, a pinch of salt, 225 ml (8 fl oz) milk and 150 ml (¼ pint) water with the 2 eggs from the recipe, until smooth.

RATATOUILLE TARTLETS

SERVES 6

Ready-made filo pastry provides a quick way of making paper-light cases.

---

3 large sheets filo pastry, halved
2 tablespoons olive oil
2 cloves garlic, thinly sliced
2 courgettes, diced
1 small aubergine, diced
1 red pepper, cored, seeded and diced
2 spring onions, chopped
125 ml (4 fl oz) passata
1 teaspoon ground coriander
salt and pepper to taste
parsley sprigs to garnish

1 Preheat oven to 200°C (400°F/Gas 6). Pile the filo sheets on top of each other and cut into quarters.

2 Line 6 deep tartlet or muffin tins with the filo, using 4 squares for each, and arranging them at different angles to give a 'ragged' effect. Bake for 10 minutes, until golden.

3 Meanwhile, heat the oil in a sauté pan, add the garlic and fry until golden. Lift out with a slotted spoon and reserve.

4 Add the courgettes, aubergine and pepper to the pan and cook over a high heat until softened. Add the spring onions, passata, coriander and seasoning. Cook for a few seconds.

5 Fill the filo cases with the ratatouille and garnish with the sautéed garlic slivers and parsley to serve.

RED ONION & OLIVE TARTLETS

SERVES 6

250 g (8 oz) packet shortcrust pastry
350 g (12 oz) red onions, thinly sliced
1 tablespoon lemon juice
50 g (2 oz) butter
25 g (1 oz) raisins
1 tablespoon sugar
1 tablespoon balsamic or red wine vinegar
25 g (1 oz) black olives, quartered
salt and pepper to taste
salad leaves to garnish

1 Preheat oven to 200°C (400°F/Gas 6).

2 Roll out the pastry on a floured surface to a 3 mm (⅛ inch) thickness. Using a 9 cm (3½ inch) pastry cutter, stamp out six rounds and use to line 6 tartlet tins.

3 Prick the pastry bases, line with foil and fill with baking beans. Bake for 10 minutes, then remove foil and beans and bake for a further 10 minutes.

4 Meanwhile toss the sliced onions in the lemon juice. Melt the butter in a pan, add the onions and raisins, cover and cook gently until softened.

5 Add the sugar, vinegar and olives and cook for a further 5 minutes. Season with salt and pepper to taste.

6 Warm the pastry cases in the oven for a few minutes and fill with the onion mixture. Serve hot, garnished with salad leaves.

SPICED VEGETABLES IN POPPADUM CUPS

SERVES 4

150 ml (¼ pint) oil
1 aubergine, cubed
2 tablespoons chopped fresh root ginger
1 teaspoon dried crushed chillies
1 teaspoon cumin seeds
397 g (14 oz) can chopped tomatoes
1 tablespoon ground coriander
1 teaspoon turmeric
397 g (14 oz) can chick peas, drained
salt and pepper to taste
2 tablespoons chopped coriander
4 poppadums
1 teaspoon garam masala
coriander sprigs to garnish

1 Heat 6 tablespoons oil in a large frying pan. Add the aubergine and fry until soft and browned. Remove and set aside.

2 Heat remaining oil in the pan, add the ginger, chillies and cumin and fry for 1 minute. Add the tomatoes, ground coriander and turmeric. Cook for 10 minutes until thickened.

3 Add 300 ml (½ pint) water, bring to the boil, then add the aubergine, chick peas, seasoning and half the chopped coriander. Cover and simmer for 15 minutes.

4 Preheat grill to medium high and grill the poppadums until golden. Remove while still soft and gently mould each one over an upturned jar or tumbler. Leave to cool.

5 Add the remaining coriander and garam masala to the vegetable mixture. Spoon into the poppadum cups and serve garnished with coriander.

CRUDITÉS WITH PEPPER DIP

SERVES 4

PEPPER DIP
2 red peppers, halved and seeded
1 clove garlic, crushed
½ red chilli, seeded
4 tablespoons olive oil
1 tablespoon chopped parsley
salt and pepper to taste

CRUDITÉS
8 asparagus spears, trimmed
1 large fennel bulb, trimmed
250 g (8 oz) cherry tomatoes
2 courgettes
1 head radicchio
50 g (2 oz) black olives

1 Preheat grill to high and grill the peppers, skin side up, until blackened and blistered. Remove and peel away the skins under running water; dry thoroughly.

2 Place the peppers in a food processor or blender with the garlic and chilli and work to a purée. With the motor running, slowly add the oil to yield a thick mixture. Add the parsley and seasoning. Transfer to a bowl.

3 Cook the asparagus in boiling salted water for 10-12 minutes, until tender. Drain and refresh in cold water.

4 Halve and slice the fennel. Slice the courgettes diagonally. Separate the radicchio leaves.

5 Arrange the vegetables and olives on a large serving platter with the dip.

WHITE GAZPACHO

SERVES 6

A pretty summer soup. Either make it well in advance to give adequate time to chill, or add a few ice cubes when serving.

2 cucumbers, peeled and diced
1 clove garlic
1 green pepper, diced
750 ml (1¼ pints) chicken stock
425 ml (15 fl oz) thick sour cream
225 ml (8 fl oz) natural yogurt
3 tablespoons white wine vinegar
2 teaspoons salt
pepper to taste

TO GARNISH
parsley sprigs
diced cucumber and green pepper
toasted flaked almonds

1 Place the cucumbers, garlic and green pepper in a food processor or blender with a little of the chicken stock. Purée until smooth, then add the remaining stock.

2 Put the sour cream and yogurt into a bowl and stir in a little of the puréed mixture to thin.

3 Stir in the remaining mixture, and add the vinegar, salt and pepper. Chill.

4 Serve garnished with parsley and accompanied by bowls of diced cucumber, green pepper and flaked almonds.

BEETROOT & FENNEL SOUP

SERVES 4

Chicken consommé gives this soup a good rich flavour, but you can use stock instead. Serve hot or chilled.

50 g (2 oz) butter
250 g (8 oz) fennel, thinly sliced
425 g (15 oz) can chicken consommé
125 ml (4 fl oz) red wine
350 g (12 oz) cooked beetroot, chopped
salt and pepper to taste
2 tablespoons chopped dill
4 tablespoons thick sour cream

TO GARNISH
dill sprigs
shredded cooked beetroot

1 Melt the butter in a pan. Add the fennel and cook gently until softened.

2 Add the chicken consommé and red wine. Bring to the boil, cover and simmer for 5 minutes. Add the beetroot and cook for 10 minutes.

3 Transfer to a food processor or blender and purée until smooth. Season and stir in the dill.

4 If serving chilled, allow the soup to cool, then chill for several hours. If serving hot, reheat gently.

5 Add a spoonful of sour cream to each serving and garnish with dill and beetroot.

CHICKEN & AVOCADO WITH BACON DRESSING

SERVES 4

A delicious blend of textures and flavours. Arrange the salad before you make the dressing, so you can apply the dressing and serve immediately, while still warm.

---

1 large avocado, halved, stoned and peeled
150 g (5 oz) cooked chicken breast, sliced

WARM BACON DRESSING
2 tablespoons olive oil
75 g (3 oz) smoked streaky bacon, derinded and
  chopped
1 tablespoon tarragon vinegar
1 tablespoon capers

TO GARNISH
tarragon sprigs

1. Slice the avocado thinly and arrange the slices alternately with the chicken, overlapping on individual plates.

2. To make the dressing, heat the oil in a frying pan and fry the bacon until golden and crisp.

3. Remove from the heat, add the vinegar and capers and immediately pour over the salad. Garnish with tarragon sprigs. Serve whilst still warm, with brown bread and butter.

CHICKEN LIVER & PEPPERCORN PÂTÉ

SERVES 6

If you want to keep this pâté for a few days, pack it into a small china serving dish, smooth the surface and pour clarified butter over the top to cover completely.

---

2 tablespoons olive oil
1 onion, chopped
250 g (8 oz) chicken livers, trimmed
2 cloves garlic, chopped
125 g (4 oz) melted butter
1 tablespoon brandy
1 tablespoon chopped parsley
1 teaspoon chopped thyme
salt and pepper to taste
1 tablespoon green peppercorns in brine, drained

TO SERVE
thyme sprigs and green peppercorns to garnish
toast fingers or melba toast

1. Heat the oil in a pan, add the onion and fry gently until softened.

2. Add the chicken livers and garlic and cook for 8-10 minutes.

3. Transfer the mixture to a blender or food processor. Add the melted butter, brandy, herbs and seasoning, and blend until smooth. Add the peppercorns and blend for a few seconds until mixture is evenly combined.

4. Spoon the pâté on to individual serving dishes and garnish with thyme and peppercorns. Serve with toast.

ABOVE: CHICKEN & AVOCADO WITH BACON DRESSING *BELOW*: CHICKEN LIVER & PEPPERCORN PÂTÉ

BACON & FRIED PASTA SALAD

SERVES 4-6

Fried pasta has an interesting taste and texture. Tossed with crisp leaves, it makes a very attractive side salad.

125 g (4 oz) ondule or pasta spirals
2 tablespoons olive oil
125 g (4 oz) streaky bacon, chopped
50 g (2 oz) pine nuts
1 teaspoon finely chopped rosemary
1 clove garlic, chopped
2 tablespoons sherry vinegar
pepper to taste
1 small head frisée (curly endive)
1-2 tomatoes, sliced
15 g (½ oz) freshly shredded Parmesan cheese

1 Bring a large saucepan of salted water to the boil. Add the pasta, stir once and boil for 10-12 minutes until tender. Drain, then refresh under cold water and drain thoroughly. Toss in a little oil to prevent sticking.

2 Heat 1 tablespoon oil in a frying pan, add the bacon and fry for about 5 minutes, until crisp. Add the pasta and fry for a further 5 minutes, turning constantly, until the pasta starts to become crisp. Add the pine nuts, rosemary and garlic and fry for 2 minutes, stirring. Add the remaining oil, the vinegar and pepper. Warm through.

3 Line individual serving plates with frisée and a few tomato slices. Spoon the pasta on top and sprinkle with Parmesan to serve.

SMOKED CHICKEN & PASTA SALAD

SERVES 4-6

175 g (6 oz) pasta bows
½ cucumber
2 carrots
2 tablespoons olive oil
2 slices bread, cubed
250 g (8 oz) smoked chicken, cubed
1 lettuce, finely shredded
mint sprigs to garnish

DRESSING
2 tablespoons natural yogurt
2 tablespoons chopped mint
1 tablespoon wine vinegar
1 tablespoon olive oil
1 clove garlic, crushed
1 teaspoon clear honey
salt and pepper to taste

1 Bring a large pan of salted water to the boil. Add the pasta, stir once and boil for 10-12 minutes until tender. Drain, then refresh under cold water. Drain well and toss in a little oil to prevent sticking.

2 Cut the cucumber and carrots into thin sticks.

3 Heat the oil in a frying pan. Add the bread and fry until crisp and golden; drain on kitchen paper.

4 Place all the dressing ingredients in a bowl and whisk together with a fork.

5 Combine the pasta, chicken, cucumber and carrots in a serving bowl. Pour over the dressing and toss well. Serve on a bed of lettuce, sprinkled with the croûtons and garnished with mint.

ABOVE: BACON & FRIED PASTA SALAD *BELOW*: SMOKED CHICKEN & PASTA SALAD

VEGETABLE COUSCOUS

SERVES 6

Couscous is a cereal processed from semolina and used in North Africa as an alternative to rice. It makes a delicious base for this sustaining spiced vegetable mixture.

3 tablespoons oil
1 teaspoon salt
500 g (1 lb) couscous
50 g (2 oz) butter
1 large onion, finely chopped
2 cloves garlic, crushed
1 tablespoon tomato purée
½ teaspoon turmeric
½ teaspoon cayenne pepper
1 teaspoon ground coriander
1 teaspoon ground cumin
250 g (8 oz) cauliflower florets
250 g (8 oz) baby carrots, trimmed
1 red pepper, cored, seeded and diced
250 g (8 oz) courgettes, thickly sliced
250 g (8 oz) baby corn
250 g (8 oz) button mushrooms, halved
3 tablespoons chopped coriander
salt and pepper to taste
coriander leaves to garnish

1 Bring 500 ml (18 fl oz) water to the boil in a large pan. Add 1 tablespoon oil and the salt. Remove from the heat, then add the couscous, stirring. Allow to swell for 2 minutes, then add the butter and heat gently, stirring to separate the grains; keep hot.

2 Heat the remaining 2 tablespoons oil in a large pan, add the onion and garlic, and fry until softened. Stir in the tomato purée, turmeric, cayenne, ground coriander and cumin. Cook, stirring, for 2 minutes.

3 Add the cauliflower, carrots and pepper and enough water to come halfway up the vegetables. Bring to the boil and simmer, covered, for 10 minutes.

4 Add the courgettes and baby corn and cook for a further 10 minutes. Add the mushrooms, chopped coriander and seasoning. Cook for 2-3 minutes.

5 Turn the couscous out on to a serving dish and spoon the vegetables on top, pouring over any extra liquid. Garnish with coriander leaves.

ARTICHOKE & SALAMI SALAD

SERVES 4

The rustic flavour of this salad will appeal to those who like strong tastes. Don't be tempted to use a cheap alternative – only Italian salami will do.

175 g (6 oz) wholewheat pasta shells
425 g (15 oz) can artichoke hearts
50 g (2 oz) Italian salami
50 g (2 oz) black olives
75 g (3 oz) button mushrooms
½ red onion, thinly sliced

DRESSING
1 tablespoon balsamic vinegar
3 tablespoons extra virgin olive oil
salt and pepper to taste

1. Bring a large saucepan of salted water to the boil. Add the pasta, stir once and boil for 10-12 minutes until tender. Drain, then refresh under cold water and drain thoroughly. Toss in a little oil to prevent sticking.

2. Drain the artichokes thoroughly, then slice thinly. Cut the salami into strips, halve the olives and slice the mushrooms and onion. Place the pasta in a large bowl with the artichokes, salami, olives, mushrooms and onion.

3. Place the dressing ingredients in a screw-topped jar and shake well to mix. Pour over the salad and toss lightly to serve.

PRAWN & PASTA SALAD

SERVES 4-6

Serve this as a pretty summer starter, or as part of a buffet meal. Other seafood such as cooked mussels, clams or squid rings can be used instead of – or in addition to – the prawns.

175 g (6 oz) pipe rigate or pasta shells
1 small head fennel
2 spring onions, chopped
1 tablespoon chopped dill
125 g (4 oz) cherry tomatoes, halved
250 g (8 oz) peeled prawns
few unshelled cooked prawns (optional)

DRESSING
2 tablespoons olive oil
1 tablespoon lemon juice
1 clove garlic, crushed
2 teaspoons finely chopped root ginger
1 teaspoon coarse-grain mustard
1 teaspoon sugar
salt and pepper to taste

1. Bring a large saucepan of salted water to the boil. Add the pasta, stir once and boil for 10-12 minutes until tender. Drain, then refresh under cold water and drain well. Toss in a little oil to prevent sticking.

2. Quarter the fennel, remove the core, then slice thinly. Place in a large bowl with the pasta, spring onions, dill, tomatoes and peeled prawns. Mix well.

3. Place all the dressing ingredients in a small bowl and whisk with a fork. Pour over the salad just before serving. Garnish with whole cooked prawns if desired.

ONION & GRUYÈRE JALOUSIE

SERVES 4-6

The top of this attractive pie is slashed to represent a venetian blind – the literal translation of the French word 'jalousie'. Ready-made puff pastry is available fresh or frozen.

---

50 g (2 oz) butter
3 large onions, thinly sliced
1 tablespoon wholegrain mustard
salt and pepper to taste
350 g (12 oz) packet puff pastry
25 g (1 oz) gruyère cheese, grated
beaten egg to glaze
2 teaspoons sesame seeds
salad leaves to garnish

1 Preheat oven to 230°C (450°F/Gas 8).

2 Melt the butter in a large pan, add the onions and cook gently until softened. Stir in the mustard and seasoning.

3 Divide the pastry into 2 pieces, one slightly larger than the other. Roll out the pastry on a floured surface to 2 rectangles, the smaller measuring about 20×13 cm (8×5 inches); the larger one measuring 25×18 cm (10×7 inches).

4 Place the smaller rectangle on a dampened baking sheet and top with the onion mixture. Spread evenly, leaving a 1 cm (½ inch) border all the way round. Sprinkle the cheese over the onion filling.

5 Dust the other pastry rectangle with flour and gently fold it in half. Using a sharp knife, cut through the folded side, at 5 mm (¼ inch) intervals, leaving a 2.5 cm (1 inch) border at the sides and top. Open out the rectangle.

6 Brush the pastry border around the onion with water, then carefully lay the cut pastry rectangle on top. Press the edges together to seal and crimp with your fingers.

7 Brush the jalousie with beaten egg and sprinkle with sesame seeds. Bake for 20 minutes, until well risen and golden brown.

8 Cut into thick slices and serve warm, garnished with salad leaves.

ICED CHICKEN & ALMOND SOUP

SERVES 4

A subtle blend of almond and chicken with juicy muscat grapes, this soup is extremely quick to make in a blender. Leave it to chill for as long as possible, or alternatively serve immediately – with a few ice cubes floating in each portion.

125 g (4 oz) cooked chicken, chopped
1 small clove garlic, crushed
125 g (4 oz) ground almonds
600 ml (1 pint) milk
salt and pepper to taste
1 teaspoon lemon juice (approximately)
125 g (4 oz) muscat grapes, halved and seeded
1 teaspoon chopped dill

1 Put the chicken, garlic, ground almonds, milk and seasoning in a blender and blend until mixture is smooth.

2 Turn into a bowl and add lemon juice to taste. Cover and chill for 30 minutes.

3 Spoon into individual soup bowls and sprinkle with the grapes and dill to serve.

Note Although you can purée this soup in a food processor, it does not give such a fine smooth texture as a blender.

CHICKEN & AVOCADO MOUSSE

SERVES 4-6

This mousse is very quick to make using a food processor, but you need to leave it to set for an hour before turning out; 15 minutes will be sufficient if you serve it in the ramekins.

125 g (4 fl oz) hot chicken stock
2 teaspoons gelatine, soaked in 2 tablespoons cold water
1 large avocado, halved, stoned and peeled
75 g (3 oz) fromage frais
1 teaspoon finely chopped spring onion
1 teaspoon lemon juice
1 teaspoon Worcestershire sauce
salt and pepper to taste
125 g (4 oz) smoked chicken, finely chopped
4 tablespoons single cream

TO GARNISH
few avocado slices
fennel sprigs

1 Add the hot stock to the soaked gelatine and stir until dissolved.

2 Roughly chop the avocado and put into a food processor with the fromage frais, spring onion, lemon juice, Worcestershire sauce and seasoning. Blend until smooth.

3 Pour into a bowl and stir in the chicken, dissolved gelatine and cream.

4 Divide between 4-6 small greased ramekins and chill for 1 hour or until set.

5 Turn out on to individual plates and garnish with avocado slices and fennel to serve.

PEPPER & AUBERGINE PIZZA

SERVES 4

290 g (10.2 oz) packet pizza base mix
125 ml (4 fl oz) passata
1 aubergine, thinly sliced
2 tomatoes, thinly sliced
1 red pepper, cored, seeded and thinly sliced
1 yellow pepper, cored, seeded and thinly sliced
1 onion, thinly sliced
2 tablespoons capers
12 black olives
50 g (1.76 oz) can anchovies, drained
2×150 g (5 oz) mozzarella cheeses
pepper to taste
olive oil for drizzling
oregano sprigs to garnish

1 Preheat oven to 220°C (425°F/Gas 7).

2 Make up the pizza base mix according to packet instructions. (For speed, use a food processor.)

3 Divide the dough into 4 equal pieces. On a floured surface, roll out each piece to a thin circle, 18 cm (7 inches) in diameter.

4 Place on lightly greased baking sheets and turn up the edges slightly.

5 Spread each one with passata, leaving a 5 mm (¼ inch) border. Top with the aubergine, tomatoes, peppers, onion, capers, olives and anchovies. Slice or chop the mozzarella and dot over the pizzas. Season with pepper and drizzle with olive oil.

6 Bake for 20 minutes until golden brown. Garnish with oregano to serve.

LEEK & GOAT'S CHEESE TART

SERVES 4-6

For a quicker method, cook the filling in the flan case without pre-baking. The pastry won't be as crisp, but is satisfactory if eaten immediately.

350 g (12 oz) packet shortcrust pastry
50 g (2 oz) butter
500 g (1 lb) leeks, thinly sliced
salt and pepper to taste
1 egg
1 egg yolk
150 ml (¼ pint) single cream
1 teaspoon dried oregano
100 g (3½ oz) mild goat's cheese
50 g (2 oz) walnut pieces

1 Preheat oven to 190°C (375°F/Gas 5).

2 Roll out the pastry on a floured surface and use it to line a 20-23 cm (8-9 inch) tart tin. Prick the base with a fork. Line with foil, fill with baking beans and bake for 10-15 minutes. Remove foil and beans.

3 Melt the butter in a large pan, add the leeks and cook until softened. Season and allow to cool for a few minutes.

4 Beat together the egg, yolk and cream. Add to the leeks with the oregano. Crumble in the goat's cheese.

5 Fill the pastry case with the leek mixture. Top with the walnuts. Bake for 20 minutes until golden.

6 Serve warm, cut into wedges, with a mixed leaf salad.

ORIENTAL CHICKEN SALAD

SERVES 4

This is a substantial salad – suitable for a light lunch.

250 g (8 oz) mangetout, topped and tailed
250 g (8 oz) baby corn, halved lengthways
350 g (12 oz) cooked chicken, cut into strips
4 spring onions, cut into julienne strips
1 red pepper, cored, seeded and cut into strips
125 g (4 oz) mushrooms, sliced
25 g (1 oz) cashew nuts, toasted

SESAME DRESSING
2 tablespoons tahini (sesame seed paste)
2 tablespoons rice or wine vinegar
2 tablespoons medium sherry
1 tablespoon soy sauce
1 teaspoon sesame oil
1 clove garlic, crushed
salt and pepper to taste

1 Blanch the mangetout and baby corn in boiling water for 3 minutes. Drain and rinse under cold water, then drain thoroughly.

2 Place in a bowl with the chicken, spring onions, red pepper and mushrooms. Toss to mix.

3 To make the dressing, put the sesame paste in a bowl and gradually mix in the vinegar and sherry. Add the soy sauce, sesame oil and garlic and mix together thoroughly, adding seasoning to taste.

4 Pour the dressing over the salad, toss well and sprinkle with the nuts to serve.

DUCK & ORANGE SALAD

SERVES 4

Boneless duck breasts are best grilled until the skin is crisp and most of the fat has run out. I like to serve the flesh slightly pink, but you can cook it for a few minutes longer than suggested if you prefer.

4 duck breasts, about 150 g (5 oz) each
oil for brushing
2 tablespoons pine nuts, toasted

ORANGE DRESSING
3 tablespoons olive oil
2 tablespoons concentrated orange juice
1 tablespoon chopped chives
salt and pepper to taste

SALAD
3 heads chicory, sliced diagonally
2 oranges, peeled and cut into segments
1 bunch watercress

1 Preheat the grill to medium. Place the duck breasts, skin side down, on a rack in the grill pan. Brush with oil and grill for 3-4 minutes. Turn the duck over and cook for 5-6 minutes until the skin has crispened.

2 Meanwhile, shake the dressing ingredients in a screw-topped jar to mix.

3 Put the salad ingredients in a bowl, pour over half of the dressing and toss well.

4 Slice the duck thinly and arrange overlapping slices on one side of each serving plate. Spoon over the remaining dressing.

5 Arrange the salad next to the duck and sprinkle with toasted pine nuts to serve.

STIR-FRIED THAI NOODLES

SERVES 4

250 g (8 oz) flat rice noodles
4 tablespoons sunflower oil
2 rashers smoked streaky bacon, diced
1 clove garlic, crushed
1 red chilli, seeded and chopped
250 g (8 oz) peeled prawns
125 g (8 oz) mooli, peeled and chopped
25 g (1 oz) creamed coconut
150 ml (¼ pint) boiling water
2 teaspoons soft brown sugar
2 tablespoons lime juice
1 tablespoon crunchy peanut butter
125 g (4 oz) beansprouts
salt to taste
6 spring onions, shredded

1. Soak the noodles in hot water for 15 minutes until soft; drain thoroughly.

2. Heat the oil in a large frying pan or wok, add the bacon and fry until crispy. Add the garlic, chilli, prawns and mooli and mix well.

3. Blend the creamed coconut with the water, then add the sugar, lime juice and peanut butter. Add to the mixture in the frying pan, stir well and simmer for 2 minutes.

4. Add the noodles, beansprouts, salt and half of the spring onions. Stir, then cook gently for 3-4 minutes, stirring occasionally.

5. Serve sprinkled with the remaining spring onions.

TAGLIATELLE WITH PRAWNS & MUSHROOMS

SERVES 4

Tiger prawns have distinctive dark pink stripes. They are now fairly easy to buy from supermarkets and fish counters. Use a mixture of green and white tagliatelle.

250-350 g (8-12 oz) tagliatelle
25 g (1 oz) butter
125 g (4 oz) button mushrooms, sliced
250 g (8 oz) tiger prawns
75 g (3 oz) curd cheese
2 tablespoons snipped chives
150 ml (¼ pint) single cream
salt and pepper to taste
25 g (1 oz) pine nuts, toasted
freshly grated Parmesan cheese to serve

1. Bring a large pan of salted water to the boil. Add the pasta, stir once and boil for 8-10 minutes until tender.

2. Meanwhile make the sauce. Heat the butter in a frying pan, add the mushrooms and fry for 2-3 minutes. Add the prawns and stir well. Add the curd cheese and stir around until it begins to melt. Add the chives, cream, salt and pepper and bring to a gentle simmer.

3. Drain the pasta and mix with the sauce. Serve sprinkled with pine nuts and accompanied by freshly grated Parmesan.

PORK WITH NOODLES & MANGETOUT

SERVES 4

Wind-dried Chinese sausages are available from oriental food stores. If you include one in this recipe, use the smaller quantity of pork.

175 g (6 oz) medium egg noodles
2 tablespoons groundnut oil
350-500 g (12 oz-1 lb) pork fillet (tenderloin), thinly sliced
1 clove garlic, crushed
2.5 cm (1 inch) piece fresh root ginger, grated
1 dried Chinese sausage, thinly sliced (optional)
4 spring onions, white part only, chopped
½ red pepper, cored, seeded and cut into diamonds
125 g (4 oz) mangetout
1 teaspoon cornflour
2 tablespoons soy sauce
2 tablespoons sherry
1 tablespoon wine vinegar
salt and pepper to taste

1 Cook the noodles in boiling water according to packet instructions. Drain.

2 Meanwhile, heat the oil in a wok. Add the pork and garlic and stir fry over a high heat for 1 minute to seal.

3 Add the ginger, Chinese sausage if using, spring onions, red pepper and mangetout to the wok and stir fry for 2 minutes.

4 Blend the cornflour with the soy sauce, sherry, vinegar and 2 tablespoons water. Add to the wok and stir until thickened. Cook for 2 minutes. Add the noodles and toss well. Season and serve at once.

ITALIAN SAUSAGE WITH GREEN LENTILS

SERVES 4

Buy fresh Italian sausages such as salamelle, salsicce and cotechino from Italian delicatessens and large supermakets. Be sure to use green or continental lentils as they can be cooked without soaking and retain their texture during cooking.

350 g (12 oz) fresh Italian-style spicy sausages
2 tablespoons virgin olive oil
1 large onion, chopped
1 stick celery, chopped
1 clove garlic, chopped
300 g (10 oz) green lentils
350 g (12 oz) tomatoes, skinned and chopped
3 oregano sprigs
150 ml (¼ pint) dry white wine
salt and pepper to taste
1 tablespoon chopped parsley

1 Prick the sausages all over with a fork and cook uncovered in a large sauté pan with a lid or wok for 3-5 minutes until lightly browned. Transfer to a plate using a slotted spoon and set aside.

2 Add the oil to the pan, then add the onion, celery and garlic and stir fry for 3 minutes until softened. Stir in the lentils, tomatoes, oregano, white wine and seasoning. Cover and cook gently for 15 minutes, stirring twice.

3 Cut the sausages diagonally into thick slices. Stir the parsley into the lentil mixture and scatter the sausages over the top. Cover and cook for 10 minutes, or until the lentils are just tender and the sausages are hot and cooked through. Serve with crusty bread.

GREEN VEGETABLE STIR FRY

SERVES 4-6

A fresh tasting mixed vegetable stir fry that can accompany any meal. For a pretty effect, remove lengthwise strips of peel from the cucumber with a canelle knife before slicing.

½ cucumber
3 tablespoons groundnut oil
1 teaspoon sesame oil
½ clove garlic, crushed
2.5 cm (1 inch) piece fresh root ginger, grated
1 stalk lemon grass (optional)
250 g (8 oz) broccoli florets, halved
1 courgette, thinly sliced
125 g (4 oz) mangetout
3 spring onions, shredded
salt and pepper to taste

1 Slice the cucumber fairly thinly and set aside.

2 Heat the oils in a wok. Add the garlic and ginger and stir fry for a few seconds. Grate the bulb end only of the lemon grass, if using, and add to the wok with the broccoli, courgette, mangetout and spring onions. Stir fry for 2-3 minutes.

3 Add the cucumber to the wok and stir fry for a few seconds to heat through. Season with salt and pepper and serve at once.

CHILLI CORN COBS WITH TOMATO

SERVES 4

Sweet chilli sauce is available in bottles – like ketchup – from supermarkets and oriental food stores. Turn this recipe into a delicious main course, if you like, by adding either strips of chicken breast or prawns.

2 tablespoons groundnut oil
2 teaspoons sesame oil
1 clove garlic, crushed
2.5 cm (1 inch) piece fresh root ginger, grated
250 g (8 oz) baby corn cobs
2 tablespoons sweet chilli sauce
1 tablespoon light soy sauce
1 tablespoon sherry
1 teaspoon sugar
4 tomatoes, skinned and cut into wedges
4 spring onions, shredded
salt and pepper to taste

1 Heat the oils in a wok. Add the garlic, ginger and corn cobs and stir fry for 3 minutes.

2 Add the remaining ingredients and stir fry for 2-3 minutes, until the corn cobs are tender. Add seasoning and serve immediately.

CHICKEN WITH REDCURRANTS

SERVES 4

Serve this with rice or a simple noodle dish, such as herb and sesame noodles.

4 chicken quarters, skinned
2 tablespoons light soy sauce
3 tablespoons groundnut oil
few drops of sesame oil
1 clove garlic, thinly sliced
2.5 cm (1 inch) piece fresh root ginger, shredded
1 red onion, cut into thin wedges
4 tablespoons redcurrant jelly
juice of 1 lemon
4 tablespoons chicken stock
50 g (2 oz) redcurrants (fresh or frozen)
salt and pepper to taste
1 tablespoon snipped chives

TO GARNISH
redcurrant sprigs and chives

1 Rub the chicken with the soy sauce and leave for 10 minutes.

2 Heat the oils in a wok or large sauté pan. Add the chicken and cook for 2-3 minutes, turning until browned all over. Remove and set aside.

3 Add the garlic, ginger and onion to the pan and stir fry for 2 minutes. Stir in the redcurrant jelly, lemon juice and stock.

4 Return the chicken to the pan, cover and simmer for 15-20 minutes, until tender, then uncover and boil rapidly to reduce the liquid.

5 Stir in the redcurrants and seasoning and cook for 1 minute. Serve, sprinkled with snipped chives. Garnish with redcurrant sprigs and chives.

DUCK WITH CALVADOS & APPLES

SERVES 4

2 tablespoons light olive oil
500 g (1 lb) boneless duck breasts, skinned and cut into strips
salt and pepper to taste
50 g (2 oz) butter
1 shallot, chopped
1 clove garlic, chopped
2 rashers streaky bacon, derinded and chopped
175 g (6 oz) whole open cup mushrooms
6 tablespoons Calvados or brandy
2 teaspoons finely chopped thyme
3 tablespoons double cream
2 dessert apples, peeled, cored and cut into thick wedges

TO GARNISH
thyme sprigs

1 Heat the oil in a wok or large sauté pan. Add the duck and stir fry for 3 minutes. Season, then remove and set aside.

2 Add half the butter to the pan and heat gently. Add the shallot, garlic, bacon and mushrooms and stir fry for 3 minutes.

3 Return the duck to the pan and add the Calvados or brandy and thyme. Cook over a fairly high heat for about 2 minutes to reduce the juices, then lower the heat and stir in the cream. Adjust the seasoning and transfer to a warmed serving plate; keep hot.

4 To prepare the apples, melt the remaining butter in a clean pan and quickly fry the apple wedges until golden brown. Arrange around the duck and garnish with thyme to serve.

OKRA WITH MUSTARD

SERVES 4-6

Okra features mainly in African, Indian, South American and West Indian cooking. Serve this dish as an accompaniment to poultry and meat dishes, especially lamb.

500 g (1 lb) okra
juice of 1 lemon
3 teaspoons mustard seeds
3 tablespoons olive oil
½ onion, chopped
2 tablespoons mild mustard
3 tablespoons single cream
salt and pepper to taste

TO GARNISH
mint sprigs

1 Top and tail the okra and place in a bowl. Add cold water to cover and half the lemon juice. Leave to stand for about 20 minutes to remove some of the sticky gum. Rinse thoroughly and pat dry.

2 Place the mustard seeds in a wok or large frying pan over moderate heat and stir for about 1 minute to release the flavour. Remove and set aside.

3 Heat the oil in the wok or pan, add the okra and onion and stir fry for 3-4 minutes until tender.

4 Add the mustard and remaining lemon juice to the pan and continue cooking for 1-2 minutes. Stir in the cream, heat gently and season.

5 Transfer to a warmed serving dish and sprinkle with the mustard seeds. Garnish with mint sprigs to serve.

SPICED PLANTAIN

SERVES 4-6

Buy your plantains from large supermarkets or Asian or West Indian stores. Select those which are well speckled with black to ensure they are ripe enough for this recipe. Serve with grilled or barbecued foods for a taste of the Caribbean!

500-625 g (1-1¼ lb) plantains
25 g (1 oz) butter
1 tablespoon olive oil
2.5 cm (1 inch) piece fresh root ginger, shredded
1 tablespoon lemon or lime juice
½-1 teaspoon mild chilli powder
salt to taste

TO GARNISH
lemon slices and thyme sprigs

1 Cut the plantains into wedges or chips approximately 5 cm (2 inches) long.

2 Heat the butter and oil in a wok or large frying pan. Add the plantains and ginger and stir fry for 4-5 minutes, until the plantains are crisp and golden on the outside and soft within.

3 Add the lemon or lime juice and chilli powder to taste and cook for 1 minute. Season with salt and serve hot, garnished with lemon slices and thyme sprigs.

SINGAPORE NOODLES

SERVES 4-6

Serve as a light meal or tasty accompaniment to oriental dishes. To make the carrot slices an attractive shape, cut lengthwise grooves along the carrot at regular intervals before slicing.

250 g (8 oz) medium egg noodles
3 tablespoons groundnut oil
1 teaspoon sesame oil
1 clove garlic, crushed
1 carrot, thinly sliced
50 g (2 oz) cooked ham, cut into strips
75 g (3 oz) peeled prawns
75 g (3 oz) frozen petits pois, thawed
6 peeled water chestnuts, sliced
3 spring onions, sliced
50 g (2 oz) bean sprouts
125 ml (4 fl oz) chicken stock
2 tablespoons soy sauce
2 teaspoons cornflour
salt and pepper to taste

1 Cook the egg noodles according to the packet instructions.

2 Meanwhile, heat the oils in a wok. Add the garlic and carrot and stir fry for 2 minutes. Add the ham, prawns, peas, water chestnuts, spring onions and bean sprouts and stir fry for 1 minute.

3 Stir in the chicken stock and soy sauce and bring to the boil. Blend the cornflour with 2 tablespoons cold water and add to the wok. Cook, stirring, until thickened.

4 Drain the noodles thoroughly and add to the wok. Heat through, tossing well. Season and serve at once.

HERB & SESAME NOODLES

SERVES 3-4

This fragrant dish of noodles dressed with sesame and herbs is a wonderfully simple accompaniment. Vary the herbs to suit your taste and menu.

175 g (6 oz) instant egg noodles
2 tablespoons sesame oil
2 tablespoons sesame seeds
½ clove garlic, crushed
2 tablespoons chopped coriander, basil or mint
  (or a mixture)
salt and pepper to taste

TO GARNISH
coriander or parsley leaves

1 Cook the egg noodles according to the packet instructions.

2 Meanwhile, heat the oil in a wok, add the sesame seeds and fry for about 30 seconds. Stir in the garlic and herbs.

3 Drain the noodles thoroughly and add to the wok. Heat through tossing well together. Season with salt and pepper and serve at once, garnished with coriander or parsley.

AUBERGINE IN OYSTER SAUCE

SERVES 3-4

If possible, use crushed Szechwan peppercorns to season this delicious dish. They impart a distinctive aromatic flavour.

1 large aubergine
1 red onion
3 tablespoons groundnut oil
2 teaspoons sesame oil
1 clove garlic, crushed
2 spring onions, sliced diagonally
2 tablespoons oyster sauce
150 ml (¼ pint) chicken stock
1 teaspoon cornflour
salt and pepper (preferably Szechwan) to taste

1 Thinly slice the aubergine. Cut the red onion into wedges and separate the layers into petals.

2 Heat the oils in a wok. Add the garlic, spring onions, aubergine and red onion and stir fry for 3 minutes. Add the oyster sauce and stock and cook for 1-2 minutes.

3 Mix the cornflour to a paste with 1 tablespoon cold water, add to the wok and stir until thickened. Cook for 2 minutes or until the aubergine is tender. Season with salt and pepper. Serve at once.

BABY CORN & MUSHROOM STIR FRY

SERVES 4

This fresh lemony stir fry is an ideal accompaniment to seafood and rich meats, such as duck and pork.

1½ teaspoons fennel seeds
250 g (8 oz) baby corn cobs
1 small red onion
350 g (12 oz) mixed mushrooms, e.g. oyster,
*   shiitake, chestnut, small cup or button*
½ cucumber
3 tablespoons groundnut oil
½ clove garlic, crushed
215 g (7 oz) can straw mushrooms, drained
½ teaspoon grated lemon rind
juice of ½ lemon
salt and pepper to taste

1 Put the fennel seeds in a wok over moderate heat and stir for 1-2 minutes until they start to pop; remove and set aside.

2 Leave small corn cobs whole; halve larger ones lengthwise. Cut the onion into wedges and separate into petals. Slice any large mushrooms, otherwise leave whole.

3 Using a canelle knife, cut grooves along the cucumber, then slice fairly thinly.

4 Heat the oil in the wok. Add the garlic and corn cobs and stir fry for 2 minutes. Add the fresh mushrooms and continue stir frying for 2-3 minutes.

5 Stir in the straw mushrooms, lemon rind and juice, onion and cucumber. Stir fry for 1 minute until the mushrooms are tender, but the other vegetables are still slightly crisp; do not overcook. Season with salt and pepper and serve at once, sprinkled with the fennel seeds.

ASPARAGUS & EGG RICE

SERVES 4

If fine asparagus is not available use the larger variety, peeling the stalks and slicing them lengthwise but leaving the tips intact. Serve as an accompaniment to fish, seafood and chicken dishes.

15 g (½ oz) butter
2 eggs, beaten
250 g (8 oz) fine asparagus
2 tablespoons olive oil
50 g (2 oz) frozen petits pois, thawed
250 g (8 oz) white rice, cooked
2 tablespoons chopped parsley or chives
salt and pepper to taste

TO GARNISH
chives

1 Heat the butter in a small saucepan. Add the eggs and scramble lightly until soft and creamy. Set aside.

2 Snap off and discard the woody ends of the asparagus. Cut into 5 cm (2 inch) lengths.

3 Heat the oil in a wok. Add the asparagus and stir fry for 2 minutes. Add the peas and stir fry for a further 1 minute.

4 Add the rice and parsley or chives, together with the scrambled egg. Heat through, stirring to prevent sticking. Add seasoning and serve garnished with chives.

EGG FRIED RICE WITH GLAZED VEGETABLES

SERVES 4-6

Glazed vegetable sticks give this simple egg fried rice a delicious sweet flavour. I like to serve it with beef recipes and hot and sour dishes.

1 large carrot
1 parsnip
2 celery sticks
40 g (1½ oz) butter
2 eggs, beaten
2 tablespoons oil
½ teaspoon soft light brown sugar
250 g (8 oz) white or brown rice, cooked
1 tablespoon chopped parsley
salt and pepper to taste

TO GARNISH
chervil or parsley sprigs

1 Cut the carrot, parsnip and celery sticks into julienne (matchstick) strips.

2 Melt 15 g (½ oz) of the butter in a small pan. Add the eggs and scramble lightly until they are soft and creamy. Set aside.

3 Heat the remaining butter and 1 tablespoon oil in a wok. Add the vegetables and stir fry for 2 minutes. Stir in the sugar and cook over a high heat for 1-2 minutes until the vegetables are tender, glazed and just beginning to brown. Transfer to a bowl and keep warm.

4 Heat the remaining 1 tablespoon oil in the wok. Add the rice and heat through, stirring to prevent sticking. Fold in the scrambled egg, parsley and glazed vegetables. Season and serve at once, garnished with chervil or parsley.

LEMON CHICKEN

SERVES 4

I find the lemon sauce pleasantly sharp with just 1 teaspoon honey, but you may prefer to add more.

4 skinless chicken breast fillets
1 egg white
1 tablespoon light soy sauce
1 tablespoon sherry
1 tablespoon cornflour
salt and pepper to taste
3 tablespoons groundnut oil
1 teaspoon sesame oil
1 clove garlic, crushed
2.5 cm (1 inch) piece fresh root ginger, chopped
3 spring onions, diagonally sliced
½ lemon, thinly sliced

SAUCE
2 teaspoons cornflour
1-2 teaspoons clear honey
2 tablespoons light soy sauce
300 ml (½ pint) chicken stock
shredded finely pared rind of 1 lemon

1 Mix together the sauce ingredients; set aside.

2 Thickly slice the chicken, then place between 2 sheets of greaseproof paper and beat with a rolling pin to flatten. Whisk together the egg white, soy sauce, sherry, cornflour and seasoning. Add the chicken and mix well.

3 Heat the oils in a wok and stir fry the chicken for 3 minutes, or until just cooked. Transfer to a serving plate; keep hot.

4 Add the garlic and ginger to the wok. Stir fry for 2 minutes. Pour in the sauce and cook, stirring, until thickened. Add the spring onions and lemon slices and cook for 1 minute. Pour over the chicken.

CHICKEN WITH BROCCOLI & GINGER

SERVES 4

Serve with egg fried rice or noodles for a simple meal. You could replace the chicken with slivers of beef or pork.

3 tablespoons groundnut oil
few drops of sesame oil
500 g (1 lb) skinless chicken breast fillets, sliced
2.5 cm (1 inch) piece fresh root ginger, grated
1 clove garlic, crushed
1 small red pepper, cored, seeded and thinly sliced
250 g (8 oz) broccoli, in small florets
4 spring onions, sliced
50 g (2 oz) salted cashew nuts
Szechuan or black pepper to taste

SAUCE
2 tablespoons dark soy sauce
4 tablespoons sherry
150 ml (¼ pint) water
1 tablespoon cornflour

1 Mix the sauce ingredients together in a small bowl and set aside.

2 Heat the oils in a wok, add the chicken and stir fry for 2 minutes. Add the ginger, garlic, red pepper and broccoli and stir fry for 3 minutes.

3 Pour in the sauce and stir fry for 2-3 minutes until thickened and the chicken and vegetables are cooked. Stir in the spring onions and cashew nuts and cook for a few seconds. Add seasoning and serve at once.

HOMEMADE PASTA

MAKES ABOUT 350 G (12 OZ)

The flavour and texture of homemade pasta is incomparable. Making pasta is a skill that takes a little practice, but you will find it easy, once you get the hang of it. Consider investing in a pasta machine, to avoid rolling and cutting the pasta yourself. You will find it quick and simple to use. If you are not using a machine, make sure you roll out the dough as thinly as possible.

250 g (8 oz) strong white bread flour
½ teaspoon salt
2 eggs, beaten
1 tablespoon olive oil

1 Sift the flour and salt on to a work surface. Make a well in the centre and add the eggs and oil. Gradually draw the flour into the eggs, using your hands, until you have a soft dough.

2 Knead the dough on a lightly floured surface for 10 minutes until smooth and silky, then wrap in foil or cling film and leave to rest for 1 hour.

3 Put the dough through your chosen setting on the pasta machine, sprinkling the shaped pasta lightly with flour to stop it becoming sticky. Alternatively, roll out the dough as thinly as possible. Cut into shapes or roll up like a Swiss roll and slice to form strips of tagliatelle.

4 Cook the pasta without delay in plenty of boiling salted water for 2-5 minutes, depending on size, until tender. Drain and serve immediately.

VARIATIONS Flavoured pastas are easy to make and particularly delicious. Serve with simple sauces.

Spinach pasta Defrost 50 g (2 oz) frozen chopped spinach, then place in a sieve and press out as much water as possible. Add the spinach to the flour with the eggs and oil. You may need to add a little extra flour if the dough feels sticky.

Red pepper pasta Grill a medium-sized red pepper, turning occasionally, until charred. When cool enough to handle, peel off the skin and discard the core and seeds. Chop the pepper roughly, then place in a food processor or blender and work to a smooth paste. Add to the flour with the eggs and oil, adding more flour if the dough seems sticky.

Basil & Parmesan pasta Add 4 tablespoons finely chopped basil and 25 g (1 oz) freshly grated Parmesan to the flour with the eggs and oil.

RIGHT: HOMEMADE SPINACH PASTA, RED PEPPER PASTA AND PLAIN EGG PASTA

HERB SAUCE

SERVES 4

The herbs I have used can be varied to taste. Tossed with tagliatelle or pasta shapes, this makes a good accompaniment to meat or game.

25 g (1 oz) butter
1 teaspoon chopped thyme
1 teaspoon chopped marjoram
3 tablespoons single cream
2 tablespoons chopped parsley
salt and pepper to taste

1 Melt the butter in a small pan, add the thyme and marjoram and stir briefly. Add the cream, parsley and seasoning. Heat through gently; do not allow to boil.

GARLIC & CHILLI SAUCE

SERVES 4

Serve this sauce on spaghetti as the Italians do, or use it to spice up stuffed pasta.

4 tablespoons olive oil
2 cloves garlic, finely chopped
1 red chilli, seeded and finely chopped
salt and pepper to taste
2 tablespoons chopped parsley

1 Heat the oil in a small pan, add the garlic and cook for 2-3 minutes, until softened. Add the chilli and fry for 2 minutes, until the garlic is lightly browned. Add seasoning and parsley, and cook for 1 minute.

SAGE & PARMESAN SAUCE

SERVES 4

Serve this wonderful sauce spooned over any plain or stuffed pasta.

50 g (2 oz) butter
16 sage leaves, torn
salt and pepper to taste
2 tablespoons freshly grated Parmesan cheese

1 Place the butter, sage and seasoning in a small pan and heat gently, stirring. Serve sprinkled with Parmesan.

QUICK PESTO

SERVES 4-6

Pesto is worth making yourself when basil is available in abundance, and that really means growing it yourself. Store pesto in small jars covered with a layer of olive oil.

25 g (1 oz) toasted pine nuts
50 g (2 oz) fresh basil leaves
3 cloves garlic, finely chopped
salt to taste
6-8 tablespoons extra virgin olive oil
25 g (1 oz) Pecorino cheese, grated
50 g (2 oz) Parmesan cheese, grated

1 Finely chop the pine nuts in a blender or clean coffee grinder; then remove. Add the basil, garlic, salt and half the oil to the blender and work until smooth. Add the cheeses and remaining oil and blend until smooth, then add the pine nuts.

ABOVE: HERB SAUCE, GARLIC & CHILLI SAUCE   CENTRE: SAGE & PARMESAN SAUCE   BELOW: QUICK PESTO

FRESH TOMATO SAUCE

SERVES 4

This sauce is only as good as the tomatoes you use, so check for flavour before cooking with them. Organic and plum tomatoes are usually reliable.

500 g (1 lb) tomatoes
1 tablespoon olive oil
1 onion, chopped
1 clove garlic, chopped
bouquet garni
1 teaspoon sugar
salt and pepper to taste

1 To skin the tomatoes, hold on a fork over a gas flame turning until the skin blisters; or immerse in boiling water for about 2 minutes, then drain. Peel off the skins, then chop the tomatoes.

2 Heat the oil in a small saucepan, add the onion and fry for 2-3 minutes, until softened. Add all the remaining ingredients and bring to the boil. Lower the heat and simmer, uncovered, for 10 minutes until thickened and pulpy. Discard the bouquet garni before serving.

NOTE:
If you prefer a smoother sauce, purée in a blender or food processor before using.

PINE NUT & CHIVE SAUCE

SERVES 4

A subtle sauce to serve with any stuffed pasta, but particularly good with ravioli.

50 g (2 oz) pine nuts, toasted
150 ml (¼ pint) single cream
2 tablespoons snipped chives
salt and pepper to taste
1 tablespoon freshly grated Parmesan cheese

1 Place half the nuts in a small pan with the cream, half the chives and seasoning. Heat gently, stirring all the time; do not boil. Stir in the Parmesan.

2 Serve sprinkled with the remaining nuts and chives.

PROSCIUTTO CREAM SAUCE

SERVES 4

Prosciutto might be expensive, but a little goes a long way. This sauce is ideal with green pasta.

15 g (½ oz) unsalted butter
25 g (1 oz) prosciutto, diced
150 ml (¼ pint) single cream
salt and pepper to taste
freshly grated nutmeg to taste
freshly grated Parmesan to serve

1 Melt the butter in a pan, add the prosciutto and fry gently for 2-3 minutes, until lightly browned. Stir in the cream and heat gently; do not boil.

2 Add pepper and nutmeg; add salt if necessary. Serve sprinkled with Parmesan.

ABOVE: FRESH TOMATO SAUCE, PINE NUT & CHIVE SAUCE BELOW: PROSCIUTTO CREAM SAUCE

RIGATONI WITH PEPPER & GARLIC SAUCE

SERVES 4

Peppers and garlic seem to have a natural affinity, and their sweet flavours are particularly good with pasta. The sauce can be made a couple of hours ahead of time if convenient.

1 red pepper
1 yellow pepper
1 green pepper
250-350 g (8-12 oz) rigatoni
4 tablespoons olive oil
3 cloves garlic, thinly sliced
1 tablespoon balsamic vinegar
salt and pepper to taste
2 tablespoons chopped parsley

1 Grill the peppers, turning occasionally, until the skins are charred. When cool enough to handle, peel off the skins. Halve the peppers, discard the seeds, then cut the flesh into thin slices.

2 Bring a large saucepan of salted water to the boil. Add the pasta, stir once and boil for 10-12 minutes until tender.

3 Meanwhile make the sauce. Heat 2 tablespoons of the oil in a pan, add the garlic and fry until softened and lightly browned. Add the remaining oil, vinegar, pepper slices, seasoning and parsley and heat through.

4 Drain the pasta and toss together with the sauce. Serve immediately.

PEPPERS STUFFED WITH ORZO

SERVES 4

Skinning the peppers before stuffing brings out their sweet taste. Orzo, or puntalette, are tiny pasta shaped like rice grains. They really absorb the flavours.

4 large peppers
250 g (8 oz) orzo
125 g (4 oz) stoned black olives, chopped
1 clove garlic, chopped
1 chilli, seeded and chopped
1 tablespoon capers, chopped
3 tablespoons chopped parsley
4 tablespoons extra virgin olive oil
salt and pepper to taste
2 tablespoons breadcrumbs
chilli slices to garnish

1 Preheat grill to high. Halve the peppers and discard the seeds. Grill, skin side up, until charred, then cool slightly and peel off the skins.

2 Meanwhile bring a large pan of salted water to the boil. Add the orzo, stir once and boil for 6-8 minutes until tender. Drain well.

3 Mix together the olives, garlic, chilli, capers and half of the parsley. Add the oil, orzo and seasoning; mix well.

4 Lay the peppers in an oiled shallow ovenproof dish and fill with the stuffing. Sprinkle with the breadcrumbs and remaining parsley.

5 Place under a moderate grill for 5-6 minutes, until the topping is crisp and the peppers are heated through. Garnish with chilli slices to serve.

CHEESY AUBERGINE PASTA PIE

SERVES 4

This dish can be assembled several hours in advance – ready to bake when needed. It is perfect for vegetarians.

500 g (1 lb) aubergines, thinly sliced
3-4 tablespoons olive oil
salt and pepper to taste
175 g (6 oz) pappardelle or fusilli
600 ml (1 pint) bottled tomato sauce
125 g (4 oz) mozzarella cheese, thinly sliced
2 tablespoons freshly grated Parmesan cheese

1 Preheat oven to 190°C (375°F/Gas 5) and preheat grill to medium high. Brush the aubergine slices with a little oil and sprinkle with salt. Grill for 3-4 minutes, until lightly browned then turn, brush again and brown the other side.

2 Bring a large pan of salted water to the boil. Add the pasta, stir once and boil for 10-12 minutes until almost tender; drain well. Toss in a little oil to prevent sticking.

3 Arrange half of the aubergine slices over the base of a buttered ovenproof dish. Pour half of the tomato sauce over them. Spread the pasta over the sauce and arrange the mozzarella on top. Sprinkle with a little of the Parmesan.

4 Cover with the rest of the aubergine slices, then the remaining tomato sauce. Sprinkle with Parmesan and drizzle a little oil over the top. Bake for 30 minutes, until bubbling and golden brown.

SPAGHETTI WITH AUBERGINES & RICOTTA

SERVES 4

If possible, use the salted version of ricotta for this dish.

1 medium aubergine
salt and pepper to taste
250-350 g (8-12 oz) spaghetti
4 tablespoons olive oil
1 onion, chopped
2 cloves garlic, chopped
397 g (14 oz) can chopped tomatoes
125 g (4 oz) ricotta cheese
handful of basil or parsley leaves
freshly grated Parmesan cheese to serve

1 Cut the aubergine lengthwise into thin slices. Place in a colander, sprinkle with salt and leave for 30 minutes. Rinse and pat dry with kitchen paper.

2 Bring a large pan of salted water to the boil. Coil in the spaghetti, stir once and boil for 10-12 minutes until tender. Drain thoroughly.

3 Meanwhile heat half of the oil in a frying pan. When very hot, add the aubergine slices and stir-fry quickly until softened and lightly browned; remove.

4 Add the remaining oil to the pan and fry the onion until softened. Add the garlic, tomatoes, salt and pepper and bring to the boil. Simmer gently for 10 minutes, add the aubergine slices and cook gently for 2-3 minutes.

5 Put the spaghetti into a warm serving dish. Add the sauce and crumble in the ricotta. Toss gently and sprinkle with basil or parsley. Serve with freshly grated Parmesan.

ABOVE: CHEESY AUBERGINE PASTA PIE *BELOW*: SPAGHETTI WITH AUBERGINES & RICOTTA

TOMATO CREAM SAUCE

SERVES 4

It's amazing how just a little touch of cream can make this simple sauce really special. Combine it with your favourite pasta for a simple supper, or add a few torn basil leaves and serve it on fresh pasta for an elegant quick starter.

25 g (1 oz) butter
1 small onion, chopped
1 small carrot, chopped
1 stick celery, chopped
397 g (14 oz) can tomatoes
½ teaspoon sugar
salt and pepper to taste
2 tablespoons double cream
2 tablespoons freshly grated Parmesan cheese
basil leaves to garnish

1 Place all the ingredients, except the cream and Parmesan, in a saucepan and bring to the boil. Lower the heat and simmer, uncovered, for about 20 minutes until thickened.

2 Transfer the sauce to a blender or food processor and purée until smooth. Return to the pan, add the cream and reheat gently. Taste and add more seasoning if necessary.

3 Serve sprinkled with Parmesan and garnished with basil leaves.

TWO MUSHROOM SAUCE

SERVES 4

Dried porcini mushrooms are available in small sachets from most delicatessens. They give this sauce a deliciously intense flavour – perfect for pasta.

15 g (½ oz) dried porcini mushrooms
1 tablespoon olive oil
1 red onion, finely chopped
1 clove garlic, chopped
350 g (12 oz) chestnut mushrooms, sliced
1 teaspoon chopped oregano
1 tablespoon tomato purée
2 teaspoons lemon juice
salt and pepper to taste
oregano leaves to garnish

1 Place the porcini in a small bowl and cover with about 150 ml (¼ pint) boiling water. Leave to soak for 30 minutes, then drain; strain the liquid and reserve. Slice the mushrooms thinly.

2 Heat the oil in a saucepan, add the onion and fry for 3-4 minutes, until softened. Add the garlic, porcini and fresh mushrooms and cook for a few minutes, stirring occasionally.

3 Add the reserved liquid, oregano, tomato purée, lemon juice, salt and pepper. Bring to the boil, lower the heat and simmer, uncovered, for 20 minutes.

4 Serve sprinkled with oregano leaves.

ORECCHIETTE WITH SWISS CHARD

SERVES 4

Small ear-shaped orecchiette have a wonderful firm texture as they are made from durum semolina. They are particularly good with vegetable sauces. When Swiss chard is out of season, use spinach leaves instead.

250 g (8 oz) Swiss chard, stalks removed
250 g (8 oz) orecchiette
4 tablespoons olive oil
1 red chilli, seeded and chopped
3 cloves garlic, finely chopped
salt and pepper to taste

1. Rinse the chard, drain thoroughly and shred.

2. Bring a large saucepan of salted water to the boil. Add the orecchiette, stir once and boil for 5 minutes. Add the chard and cook for a further 6-7 minutes until the pasta is tender.

3. Meanwhile make the sauce. Heat half of the oil in a small pan. Add the chilli and garlic and fry for 2-3 minutes, until lightly browned. Add the remaining oil and warm through.

4. Drain the pasta and chard thoroughly. Transfer to serving bowls and spoon the chilli and garlic sauce on top to serve.

SPINACH GNOCCHI WITH TOMATO SAUCE

SERVES 4

250 g (8 oz) frozen chopped spinach, defrosted
25 g (1 oz) butter
1 shallot, finely chopped
125 g (4 oz) ricotta or curd cheese
2 egg yolks
75 g (3 oz) plain flour
50 g (2 oz) Parmesan, freshly grated
freshly grated nutmeg to taste
salt and pepper to taste
1 quantity Tomato Cream Sauce (page 66)
freshly grated Parmesan to serve

1. Place the spinach in a fine sieve and press out as much water as possible, then transfer to a bowl.

2. Melt the butter in a pan, add the shallot and fry gently for 2-3 minutes, until softened. Add to the spinach with the ricotta, egg yolks, flour, Parmesan, nutmeg and seasoning. Mix thoroughly to a smooth dough. Cover and chill for 20 minutes until firm.

3. To shape the gnocchi, break off small pieces of dough and form into balls. Bring a large pan of salted water to the boil, then reduce to a simmer and add the gnocchi. Cook, uncovered, for about 5 minutes until they rise to the surface.

4. Using a slotted spoon, transfer the gnocchi to warmed serving bowls and pour over the tomato cream sauce. Sprinkle with Parmesan to serve.

PASTA TWISTS WITH FENNEL SAUCE

SERVES 4

A dash of Pernod brings out the subtle aniseed flavour of the fennel. The sauce can be made several hours before serving; it also freezes well.

25 g (1 oz) butter
1 onion, chopped
250 g (8 oz) fennel bulb
1 tablespoon Pernod
150 ml (¼ pint) white wine
150 ml (¼ pint) vegetable stock
250 g (8 oz) pasta twists
2 tablespoons single cream
salt and pepper to taste

1 Melt the butter in a small pan, add the onion and fry until softened, about 5 minutes. Meanwhile trim off the leaves from the fennel and reserve. Slice the bulb finely.

2 Add the sliced fennel to the pan, stirring well. Add the Pernod, wine and stock and bring to the boil. Cover and simmer for 15 minutes until the fennel is tender.

3 Meanwhile cook the pasta. Bring a large saucepan of salted water to the boil. Add the pasta, stir once and boil for 10-12 minutes until tender.

4 Put half of the sauce in a food processor or blender and work until fairly smooth. Return to the pan. Stir in the remaining sauce and cream. Warm through and check seasoning.

5 Drain the pasta and toss with the sauce. Serve sprinkled with the fennel leaves.

PAPPARDELLE WITH RICH MUSHROOM SAUCE

SERVES 4

Pappardelle are very wide flat noodles, which sometimes have wavy edges. You can use tagliatelle instead, but reduce the boiling time to 10-12 minutes.

1 tablespoon olive oil
2 shallots, chopped
1 clove garlic, chopped
2 rashers back bacon, chopped
250 g (8 oz) chestnut mushrooms, sliced
150 ml (¼ pint) canned consommé
3 tablespoons madeira
salt and pepper to taste
250-350 g (8-12 oz) pappardelle
2 tablespoons double cream

1 Heat the oil in a saucepan, add the shallots, garlic and bacon and fry until softened, about 5 minutes. Add the mushrooms and stir well.

2 Add the consommé, madeira and seasoning. Bring to the boil and simmer uncovered for 15 minutes, stirring occasionally.

3 Bring a large saucepan of salted water to the boil. Add the pasta, stir once and boil for 10-12 minutes until tender. Drain well.

4 Stir the cream into the sauce and pour over the pasta. Toss well to serve.

PEA & MINT SOUP

SERVES 6

50 g (2 oz) butter
1 bunch spring onions, chopped
3 tablespoons flour
900 ml (1½ pints) chicken stock
1 teaspoon salt
300 g (10 oz) frozen peas
500 g (1 lb) sugar snap peas, trimmed
600 ml (1 pint) water
8 lettuce leaves
25 g (1 oz) mint leaves
salt and white pepper to taste
125 ml (4 fl oz) cream

TO GARNISH
few lettuce leaves, shredded
mint sprigs

1. Melt the butter in a large pan. Add the spring onions and cook for 3-4 minutes until tender. Stir in the flour and cook, stirring, for 1 minute. Stir in the chicken stock, salt and frozen peas. Cover and cook for 10 minutes.

2. Transfer to a food processor or blender and purée until smooth. Return to the pan.

3. Put the sugar snaps, water, lettuce and mint leaves in a pan. Bring to the boil, cover and simmer for 15 minutes. Purée in the food processor or blender, then sieve to remove any strings.

4. Add to the spring onion and pea mixture, stir in the cream, season and reheat.

5. Serve garnished with lettuce and mint.

CURRIED PUMPKIN SOUP

SERVES 4

To cook this soup ultra quickly in the microwave, cook the onion, garlic and oil on high for 1 minute. Add the remaining ingredients, except yogurt, and cook for a further 5 minutes.

2 tablespoons oil
1 onion, chopped
1 clove garlic, crushed
1 tablespoon mild curry paste
425 g (15 oz) can pumpkin, drained
600 ml (1 pint) chicken stock
salt and pepper to taste
4 tablespoons natural yogurt
coriander sprigs to garnish

1. Heat the oil in a large pan. Add the onion and garlic, and cook until soft. Add the curry paste and cook for a few seconds, stirring.

2. Add the pumpkin and chicken stock. Stir well, season and simmer for 15-20 minutes.

3. Transfer the soup to a food processor or blender and purée until smooth. Return to the pan, check the seasoning and reheat.

4. Transfer to individual soup plates, swirl in the yogurt and garnish with coriander.

TOMATO & PIMIENTO SOUP

SERVES 4

A very quick 'storecupboard' recipe – perfect for an impromptu dinner party.

50 g (2 oz) butter
1 onion, finely chopped
2 cloves garlic, crushed
400 g (14 oz) can pimientos, drained, rinsed and
  chopped
230 g (8 oz) can chopped tomatoes
150 ml (¼ pint) red wine
600 ml (1 pint) chicken stock
salt and pepper to taste
2 tablespoons snipped chives

CROÛTONS
2 slices white bread, crusts removed
2 tablespoons oil

1 Melt half the butter in a pan. Add the onion and garlic and cook until soft.

2 Add the pimientos and tomatoes, cover and cook gently for 10 minutes.

3 Add the wine, cook for 5 minutes, then add the stock and cook for 5 minutes.

4 Transfer to a food processor or blender and purée until smooth. Return the soup to the pan, season and heat through.

5 To make the croûtons, cut the bread into small cubes. Heat the remaining butter and the oil in a frying pan, then fry the bread cubes until golden. Drain on kitchen paper.

6 Transfer the soup to individual bowls and garnish with the chives and croûtons to serve.

ROCKET SOUP WITH PARMESAN

SERVES 4-6

Rocket is a salad leaf with a superb pungent, peppery taste. Substitute watercress, if you can't obtain it.

2 tablespoons quality olive oil
2 cloves garlic, crushed
250 g (8 oz) potato, diced
175 g (6 oz) rocket, chopped
1.2 litres (2 pints) vegetable stock
salt and pepper to taste
4 tablespoons freshly grated Parmesan cheese
¼ teaspoon dried crushed chillies (optional)

1 Heat the olive oil in a large pan. Add the garlic and cook for 1 minute.

2 Add the potato and stir until coated in oil. Add the rocket, reserving a few leaves for garnish. Stir and cook for 2-3 minutes.

3 Heat the stock and add to the rocket mixture. Season with salt and pepper, cover and simmer for 20 minutes.

4 Ladle into soup bowls and sprinkle with Parmesan, and dried chilli if desired. Garnish with rocket leaves to serve.

DEEP-FRIED POTATO & SPINACH 'SANDWICHES'

MAKES 8

These little snacks can be made in advance and reheated in the oven.

750 g (1½ lb) large potatoes
1 tablespoon olive oil
2 cloves garlic, crushed
250 g (8 oz) frozen chopped spinach
2 teaspoons black olive purée
salt and pepper to taste
50 g (2 oz) feta cheese, thinly sliced
1 egg, beaten
dry breadcrumbs for coating
vegetable oil for shallow-frying

1 Cut the potatoes into 1 cm (½ inch) slices; you need 16 good ones. Cook in boiling salted water for 5 minutes; drain.

2 Heat the olive oil in a pan, add the garlic and cook for a few seconds, then add the frozen spinach and cook until soft. Add the olive purée, season and cook, stirring, until all liquid has evaporated.

3 Spread the mixture evenly on half of the potato slices. Cover with cheese and top with remaining potato slices.

4 Pour oil into a deep frying pan to a depth of 2.5 cm (1 inch) and heat.

5 Brush the sandwiches with beaten egg, then coat evenly with breadcrumbs.

6 Shallow-fry for 4-5 minutes on each side, until golden brown. Drain on kitchen paper. Serve warm, with a tomato relish.

JACKET POTATOES

SERVES 4

Quick jacket potatoes filled with ricotta and sun-dried tomatoes, which are available from larger supermarkets and Italian delicatessens.

4 medium baking potatoes
125 g (4 oz) ricotta or curd cheese
4 large sun-dried tomatoes, chopped
1 tablespoon pine nuts
2 tablespoons chopped basil
1 tablespoon olive oil
salt and pepper to taste
extra olive oil

TO GARNISH
basil leaves
radicchio leaves

1 Cook the potatoes in the microwave, allowing 10-12 minutes on high per 500 g (1 lb), turning halfway through cooking. Alternatively, bake in a preheated oven at 220°C (425°F/Gas 7) for 1 hour, then lower temperature to 200°C (400°F/Gas 6).

2 Cut a slice off the top of each potato and scoop out the flesh, leaving a 5 mm (¼ inch) shell.

3 Mash three quarters of the potato flesh with the ricotta or curd cheese, sun-dried tomatoes, nuts, basil, oil and seasoning.

4 Fill the potatoes with the stuffing and microwave on high for 3 minutes or return to the oven for 10 minutes.

5 Drizzle with a little olive oil and serve garnished with basil and radicchio.

NOODLES WITH AUBERGINE

SERVES 4-6

Serve as an accompaniment to chicken, beef, duck or lamb. Yellow bean sauce or paste and Szechwan peppercorns are available from large supermarkets and oriental food stores.

250 g (8 oz) aubergine
1½ teaspoons salt
250 g (8 oz) thread egg noodles
3-4 tablespoons groundnut oil
1 clove garlic, crushed
½ red pepper, seeded and cut into strips
227 g (8 oz) can bamboo shoots, drained
3 tablespoons yellow bean sauce
¼-½ teaspoon Szechwan peppercorns, crushed
1-2 teaspoons sesame oil

1 Cut the aubergine into strips and place in a colander or sieve. Rinse with cold water, then sprinkle with the salt. Leave to stand for 20 minutes to degorge, then rinse thoroughly and drain well.

2 Cook the egg noodles according to the packet instructions.

3 Meanwhile, heat the groundnut oil in a wok. Add the aubergine, garlic, red pepper and bamboo shoots and stir fry for 2-3 minutes until the aubergine is soft. Add the yellow bean sauce and heat through. Season with Szechwan pepper to taste.

4 Drain the noodles and toss in the sesame oil. Transfer to a warmed serving dish and top with the aubergine mixture to serve.

SCENTED LEMON NOODLES

SERVES 4

Fiery noodles with the Thai flavours of ginger, garlic, chilli and lemon grass – especially good as an accompaniment to fish and chicken dishes.

250 g (8 oz) rice noodles
3 tablespoons olive or groundnut oil
½ clove garlic, crushed
2.5 cm (1 inch) piece fresh root ginger, grated
1 large red or green chilli, seeded and thinly
  sliced
2 stalks lemon grass (see note)
3 spring onions, sliced
50 g (2 oz) salted peanuts, roughly chopped
salt and pepper to taste

1 Cook the rice noodles according to the packet instructions.

2 Meanwhile, heat the oil in a wok. Add the garlic, ginger and chilli and stir fry for 1 minute.

3 Grate the bulb end of the lemon grass. Add to the wok with the spring onions and peanuts. Continue stir frying for about 30 seconds.

4 Drain the cooked noodles and add to the wok. Heat through, tossing well together. Add seasoning. Serve immediately.

Note If lemon grass is not obtainable, substitute the grated rind and juice of ½ lemon and ½ teaspooon brown sugar.

GINGERED PARSNIP BATONS

SERVES 4

A delicious accompaniment for roast meats, poultry
and game; I particularly like to serve it with duck. As
a variation, substitute half the quantity of parsnips
with batons of carrot.

500 g (1 lb) parsnips
2 tablespoons olive oil
15 g (½ oz) butter
5 cm (2 inch) piece fresh root ginger, finely
  shredded
1 tablespoon lemon juice
½ teaspoon soft light brown sugar
salt and pepper to taste

TO GARNISH
snipped chives

1 Cut the parsnips in half across the middle, then
cut each piece lengthwise into four or six pieces
to give batons of approximately equal size.

2 Heat the oil and butter in a wok or large frying
pan. Add the ginger and parsnips and stir fry for
about 5 minutes, until the parsnips are tender.

3 Add the lemon juice and sugar to the pan and
cook for about 1 minute until the parsnips are
lightly glazed. Season with salt and pepper.

4 Transfer to a warmed serving dish and sprinkle
with snipped chives to serve.

MUSHROOMS WITH MADEIRA & GARLIC

SERVES 4

While developing recipes for a mushroom cookbook,
I became addicted to the flavour combination of
mushrooms with Madeira wine. This simple
vegetable accompaniment is best made using wild
field mushrooms, but the large cultivated flat
mushrooms available from supermarkets and
greengrocers work well too.

50 g (2 oz) butter
1 tablespoon olive oil
2 cloves garlic, thinly sliced
1 shallot, finely chopped
500 g (1 lb) large field mushrooms, thickly sliced
125 ml (4 fl oz) Madeira
1 teaspoon cornflour
salt and pepper to taste

TO GARNISH
parsley sprigs

1 Heat the butter and oil in a wok or large frying
pan. Add the garlic and shallot and stir fry for
1 minute. Add the mushrooms and stir fry for a
further 2 minutes.

2 Pour in the Madeira, cover and cook over a
medium heat for 5 minutes until the mushrooms
are tender.

3 Mix the cornflour to a paste with a little cold
water, then add to the pan. Stir until thickened.
Season with salt and pepper.

4 Transfer to a warmed serving dish and serve at
once garnished with parsley.

ABOVE: GINGERED PARSNIP BATONS *BELOW*: MUSHROOMS WITH MADEIRA & GARLIC

NOODLES WITH STIR-FRIED VEGETABLES

SERVES 4

Once the preparation is done, this dish is assembled in minutes.

250 g (8 oz) Chinese egg noodles
2 teaspoons sesame oil
2 tablespoons sunflower oil
1 clove garlic, chopped
1 leek, thinly sliced
227 g (8 oz) can water chestnuts, drained
½ red pepper, cored, seeded and chopped
175 g (6 oz) broccoli florets
1 teaspoon chilli bean sauce
2 teaspoons tomato purée
2 tablespoons dry sherry
2 tablespoons soy sauce
½ teaspoon sugar
125 g (4 oz) oyster mushrooms

1 Bring a large pan of salted water to the boil. Add the noodles, cover, remove from the heat and leave to stand for 6 minutes. Drain and toss in sesame oil.

2 Heat the sunflower oil in a large frying pan or wok. Add the garlic and leek and stir-fry for 1 minute. Add the sliced water chestnuts, pepper and broccoli and stir-fry for 1 minute.

3 Mix together the chilli bean sauce, tomato purée, sherry, soy sauce, sugar and 2 tablespoons water. Add to the pan and stir well. Cover and simmer for 2-3 minutes.

4 Stir in the noodles and mushrooms. Cover and cook for 2 minutes. Serve immediately.

BOWS WITH TOMATO & PEPPER SAUCE

SERVES 4

1 yellow pepper
2 tablespoons olive oil
1 onion, sliced
397 g (14 oz) can chopped tomatoes
1 tablespoon tomato purée
salt and pepper to taste
250-350 g (8-12 oz) pasta bows
50 g (2 oz) black olives
handful of basil leaves, torn if large
freshly grated Parmesan cheese to serve

1 Preheat the grill to high. Grill the pepper until the skin is charred, turning occasionally. When cool enough to handle, peel off the skin, discard the seeds and slice the flesh.

2 Heat the oil in a saucepan, add the onion and fry until softened. Add the tomatoes, tomato purée, yellow pepper, salt and pepper. Bring to the boil, then simmer for 15 minutes, until pulpy.

3 Meanwhile cook the pasta. Bring a large saucepan of salted water to the boil. Add the pasta, stir once and boil for 10-12 minutes until tender.

4 Stir the olives and basil into the sauce.

5 Drain the pasta and transfer to warmed serving plates. Pour the sauce over the top and serve with Parmesan.

MEXICAN CORN MUFFINS

MAKES 18

Eat these tasty muffins warm, with butter if you like. They make ideal party food, if baked in mini tins, and they freeze very successfully.

175 g (6 oz) cornmeal
175 g (6 oz) plain flour, sifted
1 tablespoon baking powder
1 teaspoon salt
1/2 teaspoon bicarbonate of soda
1/2 teaspoon sugar
1 onion, chopped
2 red chillies, seeded and chopped
1/2 red pepper, cored, seeded and chopped
2 eggs, beaten
225 ml (8 fl oz) full-fat milk
125 ml (4 fl oz) vegetable oil
125 g (4 oz) Cheddar cheese, grated
198 g (7 oz) can sweetcorn, drained

1 Preheat oven to 200°C (400°F/Gas 6).

2 In a large bowl, mix together the cornmeal, flour, baking powder, salt, bicarbonate of soda and sugar.

3 Put the onion, chillies, pepper, eggs and milk in a food processor or blender, and work to a purée.

4 Add to the dry ingredients with the oil, cheese and sweetcorn. Stir until evenly blended.

5 Spoon into greased muffin tins and bake for about 20 minutes until risen and golden. Serve immediately.

NACHOS

SERVES 6

These disappear very quickly, so make lots! Vary the toppings, including ingredients such as canned salted black beans, sliced red onions and peppers. Try different cheeses too.

30 tortilla chips
298 g (10 1/2 oz) can cream-style corn
1 avocado, diced
50 g (2 oz) Cheddar cheese, grated
2 red chillies, seeded and thinly sliced
pepper to taste
parsley sprigs to garnish

1 Preheat grill to high.

2 Arrange the tortilla chips in a single layer in a shallow ovenproof dish.

3 Put a heaped teaspoon of creamed corn on each one and top with the avocado. Sprinkle with the cheese and chilli slices and season with pepper.

4 Cook under the grill for 2-3 minutes until the cheese melts. Serve immediately, garnished with parsley.

SPINACH RICE PILAF

SERVES 6

This pilaf makes a perfect accompaniment to Indian dishes, such as curries or other spiced foods. Turn it into a meal in itself by adding cooked chopped chicken or prawns, 5 minutes before the end of cooking.

350 g (12 oz) basmati rice
2 tablespoons vegetable oil
1 large onion, finely chopped
350 g (12 oz) frozen chopped spinach, defrosted
 and squeezed dry
50 g (2 oz) raisins
50 g (2 oz) unsalted cashew nuts, roughly
 chopped
juice of ½ lemon
salt and pepper to taste
chervil or parsley sprigs to garnish

1 Wash and rinse the basmati rice several times to remove the starch.

2 Heat the oil in a heavy-based pan, add the onion and cook until softened. Add the rice and cook, stirring, until translucent.

3 Add the spinach, raisins and nuts, then stir in 450 ml (¾ pint) water. Bring to the boil, cover and simmer until the water is absorbed and the rice is fluffy. Top up with more water if necessary, during cooking.

4 Add the lemon juice and seasoning. Garnish with chervil or parsley to serve.

CORN & PIMIENTO FRITTERS

SERVES 6

These American-style fritters are traditionally served with fried chicken.

140 g (4½ oz) plain flour
pinch of salt
2 eggs, 1 separated
225-275 ml (8-10 fl oz) milk
1 tablespoon oil
vegetable oil for shallow-frying
283 g (10 oz) can sweetcorn, drained
½ small red pepper, cored, seeded and finely
 chopped
salt and pepper to taste
parsley sprigs to garnish

1 Sift the flour and salt into a large mixing bowl and make a well in the centre. Add 1 whole egg, plus 1 egg yolk. Mix to a smooth paste.

2 Gradually add the milk and beat until creamy. Stir in the oil.

3 Heat the vegetable oil in a deep frying pan to 190°C (375°F).

4 Whisk the egg white until stiff, then fold into the batter. Fold in the sweetcorn, red pepper and seasoning.

5 Drop large spoonfuls of the mixture into the hot oil and fry for 2 minutes on each side, until puffed and golden.

6 Drain on kitchen paper and serve immediately, garnished with parsley.

STIR-FRIED BEEF WITH NOODLES

SERVES 4

Once you have all the ingredients assembled and prepared, this dish takes only a few minutes to cook. It works equally well with chicken and pork. To make it easier to cut the meat into wafer-thin slices, wrap it in freezer wrap and freeze for 30 minutes before slicing.

---

250 g (8 oz) broccoli
350 g (12 oz) skirt of beef
2 tablespoons dry sherry
2 tablespoons soy sauce
2 teaspoons cornflour
250 g (8 oz) Chinese egg noodles
4 tablespoons sunflower oil
1 clove garlic, crushed
1 teaspoon grated fresh root ginger
1 onion, thinly sliced
125 g (4 oz) mushrooms, thinly sliced
300 ml (½ pint) boiling water
125 g (4 oz) beansprouts
2 spring onions, sliced diagonally

1 Break up the broccoli florets into small pieces, then slice the stalks thinly on the diagonal.

2 Slice the beef as thinly as possible across the grain, then place in a bowl with the sherry, soy sauce and cornflour. Stir well to coat evenly.

3 Bring a large saucepan of salted water to the boil. Add the noodles, remove from the heat, cover and leave for 6 minutes. Drain well and toss in a little oil.

4 Meanwhile, heat half the oil in a large frying pan or wok. Add the garlic and ginger and stir-fry for 1 minute. Add the onion and stir-fry for 1 minute. Add the broccoli and mushrooms and stir-fry for 1 minute. Remove all the vegetables from the pan with a slotted spoon and transfer to a plate.

5 Add the remaining oil to the pan. When it is hot, add the meat and stir-fry quickly until browned, about 2 minutes. Add the boiling water and bring to the boil, stirring. Return the vegetables to the pan, stir well and cook for 1 minute.

6 Add the beansprouts and noodles, bring to the boil, then cover and cook for 2 minutes.

7 Serve immediately, sprinkled with the spring onions.

MUSHROOM & CHICKEN GOUGÈRE

SERVES 4

A classic dish from Burgundy in France. The gougère mixture can alternatively be baked in spoonfuls, and eaten as a snack with a glass of wine.

GOUGÈRE
175 ml (6 fl oz) water
65 g (2½ oz) butter
100 g (3½ oz) plain flour, sifted
½ teaspoon salt
3 eggs, beaten
50 g (2 oz) Gruyère or Cheddar cheese, grated

FILLING
25 g (1 oz) butter
1 onion, finely sliced
75 g (3 oz) flat or brown mushrooms, sliced
300 ml (½ pint) ready-to-use béchamel sauce
350 g (12 oz) cooked chicken, diced
1 tablespoon chopped parsley
salt and pepper to taste

TO GARNISH
parsley sprigs

1 Preheat oven to 200°C (400°F/Gas 6).

2 To make the gougère, put the water and butter in a large pan and heat gently until the butter has melted. Bring to the boil, remove from the heat and immediately add the flour and salt, stirring continuously, until the mixture is smooth and leaves the sides of the pan.

3 Gradually beat in the eggs, a little at a time, until the mixture is smooth, shiny and drops fairly easily from the spoon. Stir in the cheese and season with salt and pepper.

4 Spoon the mixture around the edge of a greased 23-25 cm (9-10 inch) gratin dish. Bake for 25-30 minutes, until puffed and golden.

5 To make the filling, melt the butter in a pan, add the onion and cook until softened. Add the mushrooms and cook for 1 minute. Stir in the béchamel sauce, then the chicken and parsley. Simmer for 5 minutes. Season with salt and pepper.

6 Fill the gougère ring with the chicken mixture. Serve cut into wedges and garnished with parsley.

CREOLE PRAWN GUMBO

SERVES 6

This tasty Creole dish is a cross between a stew and a soup. It is traditionally served with rice. The most important ingredient is okra, a bright green seed pod, which gives the dish its characteristic silky texture. Use fresh or defrosted frozen prawns.

---

125 g (4 oz) butter
60 g (2½ oz) plain flour
1 onion, chopped
1 green pepper, cored, seeded and chopped
2 spring onions, chopped
1 tablespoon chopped parsley
1 clove garlic, crushed
1 beef tomato, chopped
100 g (3½ oz) garlic sausage, finely chopped
500 g (1 lb) okra, sliced
1 bay leaf
1 teaspoon thyme
2 teaspoons salt
pepper to taste
pinch of cayenne pepper
2 teaspoons lemon juice
4 cloves
500 g (1 lb) large shelled prawns

TO SERVE
plain boiled rice

1 Heat the butter in a large heavy-based pan. Add the flour and cook, stirring, until lightly browned.

2 Add the onion, pepper, spring onions, parsley and garlic. Cook, stirring, for about 5 minutes, until lightly browned.

3 Add the tomato and garlic sausage and mix thoroughly. Pour in 1.2 litres (2 pints) water, then add the okra, bay leaf, thyme, salt and pepper, cayenne, lemon juice and cloves. Cover and simmer for 20 minutes.

4 Add the prawns and cook for a further 2 minutes to heat through. Stir in a little more water if the mixture is too thick.

5 Serve piping hot in deep bowls, ladled over plain boiled rice.

PORK WITH PEANUT SAUCE

SERVES 4

Strips of pork and red pepper in a rich peanut sauce. Serve with rice or orso – tiny rice-shaped pasta – and a simple salad.

3 tablespoons groundnut oil
500 g (1 lb) boneless pork steaks, cut into strips
1 onion, chopped
1 red pepper, cored, seeded and thinly sliced
1 clove garlic, crushed
2.5 cm (1 inch) piece fresh root ginger, grated
2 teaspoons ground coriander
½-1 teaspoon ground cumin
2 tablespoons soft dark brown sugar
grated rind and juice of 1 lemon
4 tablespoons crunchy peanut butter
3 tablespoons dark soy sauce
1 tablespoon Worcestershire sauce
salt and pepper to taste

TO GARNISH
chopped parsley or coriander

1 Heat the oil in a wok or sauté pan. Add the pork and stir fry for 1-2 minutes to seal. Add the onion, red pepper, garlic, ginger and spices and cook for a further 3 minutes, stirring constantly.

2 Add the remaining ingredients to the pan and stir well to mix. Lower the heat, cover and simmer for about 20 minutes until the pork is tender.

3 Serve sprinkled with parsley or coriander.

CHILLI PORK

SERVES 4

A South American style dish – best served with rice and a green vegetable. Fried plantain makes a delicious accompaniment.

3 tablespoons groundnut oil
625 g (1¼ lb) pork fillet (tenderloin), cubed
1 small onion, chopped
1 clove garlic, crushed
2.5 cm (1 inch) piece fresh root ginger, grated
2 teaspoons mild chilli powder
½ teaspoon paprika
2 thyme sprigs
1 tablespoon plain flour
2 tablespoons tomato purée
150 ml (¼ pint) hot stock
salt and pepper to taste

TO GARNISH
herb sprigs

1 Heat the oil in a wok or sauté pan. Add the pork and stir fry for 1-2 minutes to seal. Add the onion, garlic, ginger, chilli powder, paprika and thyme and continue stir frying for 2 minutes, or until the onion is softened.

2 Add the flour to the pan and cook for 2 minutes, stirring constantly. Stir in the tomato purée and remove from the heat. Gradually stir in the stock. Return to the heat and cook, stirring constantly, until the sauce is smooth and thickened. Cover and cook gently for 15 minutes.

3 Discard the thyme and check the seasoning before serving, garnished with herbs.

CHILLI BEAN & SAUSAGE CASSEROLE

SERVES 4

A hearty mixture of black eye beans and spicy sausage makes this one-pot dish a perfect supper for a cold winter's night.

2 tablespoons olive oil
1 onion, chopped
2 cloves garlic, crushed
1 small red pepper, cored, seeded and chopped
397 g (14 oz) can chopped tomatoes
1 tablespoon tomato purée
2 tablespoons canned chopped green chillies
1 tablespoon treacle
1 tablespoon dark soft brown sugar
1 bay leaf
salt and pepper to taste
250 g (8 oz) chorizo or other spicy sausage,
    thickly sliced
435 g (15 oz) can black eye beans, drained
2 tablespoons chopped parsley

1 Heat the oil in a heavy-based pan. Add the onion, garlic and pepper and cook until softened and golden.

2 Add the tomatoes, tomato purée, chillies, treacle, brown sugar, bay leaf and seasoning. Cover and simmer for 15 minutes.

3 Add the chorizo and drained black eye beans, cover and cook for a further 5 minutes. Check the seasoning.

4 Sprinkle with chopped parsley and serve with potatoes or crusty bread.

POT-AU-FEU

SERVES 4-6

2 small red onions
8 cloves garlic, unpeeled
4 carrots
1 celery heart
4 small leeks, trimmed
1 bouquet garni
1 cinnamon stick
1/2 cauliflower, cut into florets
4 large spring onions, trimmed
125 g (4 oz) French beans, trimmed
2 courgettes, quartered lengthwise
125 ml (1 1/4 pint) white wine
125 g (4 oz) frozen petits pois
4 tomatoes, skinned and quartered
1/2 teaspoon chilli paste
salt and pepper to taste

1 Simmer the red onions and garlic in boiling water for 20 minutes.

2 Meanwhile, cook the carrots, celery and leeks, with the bouquet garni and cinnamon in sufficient boiling salted water to cover for 5 minutes. Add the cauliflower, spring onions, beans and courgettes and cook for 4 minutes.

3 Drain the onions and garlic, reserving 125 ml (1/4 pint) liquid. Peel the garlic and quarter the red onions. Add to the vegetables with the wine, reserved liquor, petit pois, tomatoes, chilli paste and seasoning. Simmer for 2 minutes.

4 Serve with boiled potatoes or rice.

CHEESE PASTA SOUFFLÉ

SERVES 4-6

Don't be nervous of making this soufflé – it is
virtually foolproof!

75 g (3 oz) pasta shells or twists
250 g (8 oz) spinach
50 g (2 oz) butter
125 g (4 oz) back bacon, chopped
50 g (2 oz) plain flour
450 ml (¾ pint) milk
3 eggs, separated
freshly grated nutmeg
75 g (3 oz) mature Cheddar cheese, grated
2 tablespoons freshly grated Parmesan cheese
salt and pepper to taste

1 Preheat oven to 190°C (375°F/Gas 5). Bring a
large pan of salted water to the boil. Add the
pasta, stir once and boil for 5 minutes. Add the
spinach, and cook for a further 3-5 minutes, until
tender. Drain well.

2 Melt the butter in a large pan and fry the bacon
for 5 minutes, until lightly browned. Stir in the
flour and cook for 1 minute. Gradually stir in the
milk, cooking until thickened and smooth. Simmer
for 1 minute.

3 Remove from heat and stir in the egg yolks,
nutmeg, pasta and spinach, Cheddar, half the
Parmesan and seasoning. Whisk egg whites until stiff
and fold in.

4 Turn into a buttered 1.8 litre (3 pint) soufflé dish
and sprinkle with remaining cheese. Bake for
25-30 minutes until well risen and golden brown.
Serve immediately.

MACARONI & VEGETABLE CHEESE

SERVES 4-6

Use whatever vegetables you have to hand. An ideal
recipe for using up small quantities.

250 g (8 oz) macaroni
250 g (8 oz) carrots, sliced
125 g (4 oz) French beans, cut into pieces
250 g (8 oz) cauliflower florets
1 leek, sliced
300 ml (½ pint) milk
40 g (1½ oz) butter
40 g (1½ oz) plain flour
2 teaspoons coarse-grain mustard
salt and pepper to taste
125 g (4 oz) mature Cheddar cheese, grated

1 Preheat the oven to 200°C (400°F/Gas 6). Bring a
large saucepan of salted water to the boil. Add
the macaroni, stir once and boil for 10-12 minutes
until tender.

2 Meanwhile cook the vegetables in salted water to
cover for 8-10 minutes, until just tender. Drain,
reserving 300 ml (½ pint) cooking liquid. Drain the
macaroni thoroughly and mix with the vegetables in a
buttered ovenproof dish.

3 Warm the milk. Melt the butter in a pan, add the
flour and cook for 1 minute. Add the milk and
vegetable stock and whisk over a moderate heat until
thickened and smooth. Add the mustard and
seasoning. Simmer for 1 minute. Remove from heat
and stir in half of the cheese.

4 Pour the sauce over the pasta and sprinkle with
remaining cheese. Bake for 15-20 minutes, until
golden brown and bubbling.

ARTICHOKE RISOTTO

SERVES 4

Short-grained Arborio rice is always used for risotto. It gives a delicious creamy texture.

125 g (4 oz) butter
2 shallots, finely chopped
300 g (10 oz) Arborio rice
5 tablespoons white wine
600 ml (1 pint) vegetable stock
397 g (14 oz) can artichoke hearts, drained and
*   quartered*
1 tablespoon chopped chervil
1 tablespoon chopped parsley
25 g (1 oz) freshly grated Parmesan cheese
chervil sprigs to garnish

1 Melt 50 g (2 oz) butter in a pan, add the shallots and fry gently until softened.

2 Add the rice, stirring, until all the grains are coated in butter. Pour in the white wine and bring to the boil. Cook until the volume of liquid is reduced by half.

3 Lower the heat and add a little of the vegetable stock. Stir until the rice has absorbed all the liquid before adding any more. Continue adding liquid in small amounts in this way until the rice is cooked and creamy in texture.

4 Stir in the artichoke hearts, and cook for a few seconds to heat through. Season.

5 Stir in the remaining butter and the Parmesan. Add the chopped herbs and serve immediately, garnished with chervil.

PRAWN & MANGETOUT STIR-FRY

SERVES 4

If raw prawns are unavailable, use defrosted frozen cooked prawns, adding them at the end with the beansprouts, to avoid overcooking.

2 tablespoons vegetable oil
1 clove garlic, finely chopped
1 tablespoon chopped fresh root ginger
250 g (8 oz) raw peeled prawns
125 g (4 oz) mangetout, strings removed
125 g (4 oz) beansprouts
125 ml (4 fl oz) vegetable stock
1 tablespoon red wine vinegar
juice of 1 lime
salt and pepper to taste
lime slices to garnish

1 Heat the oil in a wok or large frying pan. Add the garlic and ginger and stir-fry for about 30 seconds.

2 Add the prawns and stir-fry for 30 seconds, then add the mangetout and cook, stirring, for a further 30 seconds.

3 Add the beansprouts, stock, vinegar and lime juice. Cook over a medium heat until the vegetables are just cooked.

4 Season and serve immediately, garnished with lime slices.

ABOVE: ARTICHOKE RISOTTO *BELOW*: PRAWN & MANGETOUT STIR-FRY

TERIYAKI TURKEY

SERVES 4

For this dish you need bamboo satay sticks. Soak them in water before use, to prevent them catching under the grill.

---

500 g (1 lb) turkey strips

MARINADE
3 tablespoons soy sauce
2 tablespoons sherry
2 cloves garlic, crushed
2.5 cm (1 inch) piece fresh root ginger, finely chopped
1 tablespoon sesame oil

FRIED RICE
2 tablespoons sunflower oil
6 spring onions, chopped
2 teaspoons ground cumin
500 g (1 lb) cooked rice

1 Mix the marinade ingredients together in a shallow dish. Add the turkey strips, turn to coat and leave to marinate for 30 minutes.

2 To make the fried rice, heat the oil in a frying pan and stir fry the spring onions for 2 minutes. Add the cumin and fry, stirring, for 1 minute. Add the rice and turn to coat with the spiced oil. Heat through gently, stirring. Cover and keep warm.

3 Preheat the grill to high. Thread the turkey on to bamboo satay sticks to resemble snakes, using about 3 strips to each stick. Grill for about 2 minutes on each side. Serve with the fried rice, and accompanied by a salad.

SWEET & SOUR CHICKEN

SERVES 4

2 tablespoons wine vinegar
1 tablespoon clear honey
1 tablespoon soy sauce
2 tablespoons tomato ketchup
1 tablespoon cornflour
salt and pepper to taste
200 g (7 oz) can pineapple chunks in syrup
2 tablespoons groundnut oil
350 g (12 oz) boneless chicken breast, cut into chunks
2 cloves garlic, chopped
1 red pepper, cored, seeded and cut into 2.5 cm (1 inch) squares
1 green pepper, cored, seeded and cut into 2.5 cm (1 inch) squares
1 onion, chopped

1 In a bowl mix together the vinegar, honey, soy sauce, tomato ketchup, cornflour and seasoning until smooth. Drain the pineapple and set aside, reserving the syrup; make up to 175 ml (6 fl oz) with water, then add to the bowl.

2 Heat the oil in a pan and stir fry the chicken for 3-4 minutes until golden. Remove from the pan.

3 Add the garlic, peppers and onion to the pan and stir fry for 4 minutes.

4 Add the cornflour mixture with the chicken and pineapple and cook, stirring, until thickened. Simmer for 3 minutes. Serve with boiled rice.

CALEDONIAN SALMON WITH GINGERED VEGETABLES

SERVES 4

Fresh salmon fillet steamed over a bed of stir fried vegetables and slivers of ginger is a perfectly simple yet delicious special occasion main course. Caledonian fillets are thick slices of salmon fillet – boneless and skinned – which are available from large supermarkets. Alternatively, you can use salmon steaks for this recipe but you will need a pan large enough to take 4 steaks in one layer, and to increase the cooking time by a minute or two.

6 tablespoons groundnut oil
2 teaspoons sesame oil
½ clove garlic, crushed
5 cm (2 inch) piece fresh root ginger, thinly sliced
pinch of Chinese five-spice powder
350 g (12 oz) small baby carrots, halved
  lengthwise
1 fennel bulb, cut into strips
1 courgette, cut into strips
3 spring onions, sliced
227 g (8 oz) can bamboo shoots, drained and
  sliced
2 tablespoons light soy sauce
pinch of sugar
1 tablespoon chopped coriander leaves
4 Caledonian salmon fillets, each about 175 g
  (6 oz)
salt and pepper to taste
4 tablespoons sherry

1 Heat the oils in a large frying pan or wok. Add the garlic, ginger, five-spice powder, carrots, fennel, courgette, spring onions and bamboo shoots and stir fry for 1 minute. Stir in the soy sauce, sugar and coriander.

2 Arrange the salmon in one layer on top of the vegetables, season with salt and pepper and spoon over the sherry. Cover with a tight fitting lid and cook over a medium heat for 7-8 minutes until the fish is opaque and cooked; do not overcook.

3 Carefully transfer the salmon to warmed serving plates and surround with the vegetables. Spoon the juices over and serve at once, accompanied by crusty bread.

CHICKEN RICE NOODLES

SERVES 4

250 g (8 oz) chicken thighs
3 slices fresh root ginger
4 cloves garlic
5 spring onions, chopped
1.2 litres (2 pints) water
1 teaspoon salt
250 g (8 oz) rice noodles
2 tablespoons soy sauce
2 tablespoons dry sherry
175 g (6 oz) carrots, thinly sliced
125 g (4 oz) shitake mushrooms, sliced
250 g (8 oz) spinach leaves, shredded
pepper to taste

1 Place the chicken in a large pan with the ginger, garlic, half the spring onions, the water and salt. Bring slowly to the boil, skim, then partly cover and simmer for 20 minutes.

2 Meanwhile, put the rice noodles in a bowl and pour on boiling water to cover. Leave to soak for 15 minutes until softened.

3 Strain the chicken stock and return to the pan. Add the soy sauce and sherry and bring to a simmer. Skin the chicken and strip the meat from the bones. Cut the meat into thin strips and add to the stock with the carrots. Simmer for 5 minutes.

4 Drain the noodles and add to the pan with the mushrooms, spinach and pepper. Simmer for 2 minutes. Serve in bowls, sprinkled with the reserved spring onions.

CHINESE NOODLES WITH PORK

SERVES 4

250 g (8 oz) pork fillet, finely sliced
2 tablespoons soy sauce
2 tablespoons cornflour
5 spring onions, shredded
250 g (8 oz) Chinese egg noodles
4 tablespoons sunflower oil
1 teaspoon chopped fresh root ginger
75 g (3 oz) baby corn, halved lengthwise
75 g (3 oz) mangetout, trimmed
175 g (6 oz) mushrooms, sliced
50 g (2 oz) canned bamboo shoots, sliced
1 tablespoon tomato purée
1 tablespoon dry sherry

1 Mix the pork with 1 tablespoon soy sauce, the cornflour and half the spring onions in a bowl.

2 Bring a large pan of salted water to the boil. Add the noodles, cover and leave to stand off the heat for 6 minutes. Drain well.

3 Heat 2 tablespoons oil in a large frying pan or wok. Add the pork and stir-fry for 1-2 minutes, until lightly browned; remove.

4 Add the remaining oil to the pan and, when hot, add the ginger, corn, mangetout, mushrooms and bamboo shoots. Stir-fry for 1 minute.

5 Blend the remaining soy sauce with the tomato purée, sherry and 5 tablespoons water. Add to the pan with the pork. Stir, then cover and cook for 3-4 minutes, until the pork is tender.

6 Add the noodles, toss well and heat through. Serve sprinkled with the remaining spring onions.

ABOVE: CHICKEN RICE NOODLES *BELOW*: CHINESE NOODLES WITH PORK

CARROT RIBBONS WITH MUSTARD SEEDS

SERVES 4

Black mustard seeds impart their flavour when heated in oil. You can use poppy seeds instead, but don't heat them.

500 g (1 lb) carrots
1 tablespoon vegetable oil
1 teaspoon black mustard seeds
1 tablespoon sesame oil
parsley or chervil sprigs to garnish

1 Using a potato peeler, pare long ribbons along the length of each carrot. Prepare as many ribbons as possible, dropping them into a bowl of iced water as you do so to enable them to curl.

2 Drain, then place in a steamer basket or sieve over a pan of boiling water. Steam, covered, for 8-10 minutes until tender, but retaining a slight crunch.

3 Heat the vegetable oil in a small pan, add the black mustard seeds and continue to heat until the seeds start to pop. Immediately pour over the carrot ribbons. Add sesame oil and toss well.

4 Serve hot or cold, garnished with parsley or chervil.

FRENCH BEAN BUNDLES

SERVES 4

A pretty way of serving beans – perfect for a smart dinner party. As an alternative, serve cold tossed in vinaigrette with a platter of cold meats.

250 g (8 oz) French beans, trimmed
1 long carrot
25 g (1 oz) melted butter
few thyme sprigs

1 Divide the French beans into 4 equal portions.

2 Using a potato peeler, pare 4 long strips of carrot. Lay each one flat and place a bundle of beans on top. Carefully tie the carrot ribbon around the beans.

3 Transfer the bean bundles to a steaming basket or sieve over a pan of boiling water. Steam, covered, for 10 minutes.

4 Using a spatula, gently lift the bundles out and place on a serving dish. Drizzle with melted butter, garnish with thyme and serve immediately.

SAUTÉED CHERRY TOMATOES WITH HERBS

SERVES 4

Don't confine cherry tomatoes to salads – cooked in this way, they make a delicious accompaniment to grilled meats. If the yellow variety is available, use a mixture of the two colours.

40 g (1½ oz) butter
1 small red onion, finely sliced
2 spring onions, sliced
1 teaspoon dill
1 teaspoon chopped parsley
275 g (9 oz) cherry tomatoes
salt and pepper to taste
parsley sprigs to garnish

1 Melt the butter in.a sauté pan. Add the red onion, spring onions, dill and parsley. Cook gently, stirring, for 5 minutes.

2 Add the cherry tomatoes and sauté for 5 minutes, until their skins are beginning to split. Season with salt and pepper.

3 Serve immediately, garnished with parsley sprigs.

SUGAR SNAPS WITH COCONUT & CHILLI BUTTER

SERVES 4

The tasty flavoured butter in this recipe can be used with a variety of vegetables – try it with French beans, broccoli, baby corn, or a mixture of these.

50 g (2 oz) butter, softened
1 small red chilli, seeded and finely chopped
1 spring onion, finely chopped
grated rind of ½ lime
25 g (1 oz) creamed coconut
350 g (12 oz) sugar snaps, strings removed

1 Melt 15 g (½ oz) of the butter in a small pan. Add the chilli and spring onion and cook until softened. Add the lime rind and creamed coconut, stirring until the coconut has dissolved. Remove from the heat.

2 Leave to cool for about 10 minutes, then beat into the remaining butter. Pack into a small bowl and place in the freezer for 5 minutes.

3 Cook the sugar snaps in boiling salted water for 5 minutes; drain.

4 Using a melon baller, scoop the flavoured butter into balls.

5 Place the sugar snaps in a warmed serving dish and dot with the butter balls. Serve immediately.

MINTED ONION IN TOAST CUPS

SERVES 6

These little tarts make a smart accompaniment to roast lamb.

6 slices of white bread
75 g (3 oz) butter
1 large onion, finely chopped
2 tablespoons chopped mint
salt and pepper to taste
mint leaves to garnish

1 Preheat oven to 200°C (400°F/Gas 6).

2 Remove the crusts from the bread and cut a 6 cm (2½ inch) square from each slice. Flatten each one with a rolling pin.

3 Melt 25 g (1 oz) of the butter and use to brush both sides of the bread squares. Line 6 tartlet tins with the bread squares, pressing in firmly. Bake for 10-12 minutes, until golden.

4 Meanwhile, melt the remaining butter with 3 tablespoons water. Add the onion and cook gently, covered, for about 10 minutes until softened. Transfer to a food processor, add the mint and work to a purée. Season with salt and pepper.

5 Fill the toast cups with the onion and mint purée. Garnish with mint leaves to serve.

ROAST VEGETABLES WITH GREMOLATA

SERVES 4

Gremolata is an Italian mixture of flat-leaved parsley, garlic and lemon rind. It gives these vegetables a delicious flavour. Use flat-leaved parsley rather than the curly variety if possible.

125 g (4 oz) small new potatoes
1 red pepper, quartered lengthwise and seeded
1 aubergine, thickly sliced
2 courgettes, halved lengthwise
4 tablespoons olive oil
1 tablespoon coarse sea salt
pepper to taste

GREMOLATA
2 cloves garlic
grated rind of 1 lemon
2 tablespoons chopped parsley

1 Preheat oven to 200°C (400°F/Gas 6).

2 Place all the vegetables in a roasting tin. Pour over the olive oil and sprinkle with the sea salt. Roast in the oven for 30 minutes, basting occasionally with the oil, until tender and lightly browned.

3 For the gremolata, mix together the garlic, lemon rind and parsley.

4 Transfer the vegetables to a warmed serving dish, season with pepper and sprinkle with the gremolata.

BROAD BEANS WITH MUSHROOMS & BACON

SERVES 4

You can use frozen broad beans if fresh ones are out of season. If they are large, it's worth peeling them – the skins can be tough, and they're a very pretty green underneath.

250 g (8 oz) broad beans
4 rashers streaky bacon, derinded
4 tablespoons olive oil
250 g (8 oz) button mushrooms, halved
salt and pepper to taste
1 tablespoon chopped chives
parsley sprigs to garnish

1. Cook the broad beans in boiling salted water for 7-8 minutes. Drain and plunge into cold water. Peel, if necessary.

2. Cut the bacon into strips. Heat the oil in a sauté pan, add the bacon and mushrooms and cook for 2 minutes. Add the broad beans and cook, stirring, for 2 minutes until heated through. Season with salt and pepper.

3. Transfer to a serving dish and sprinkle with chives. Garnish with parsley to serve.

GLAZED RADISHES

SERVES 4

We usually think of eating radishes raw, but cooking them in this way gives a mellow flavour and turns them a delicate pink colour. Serve with roast meats and game.

2 bunches of radishes, trimmed, about 325 g
   (11 oz) trimmed weight
15 g (¹/₂ oz) butter
1 teaspoon sugar
salt and pepper to taste
chervil or parsley sprigs to garnish

1. Put the radishes, butter and sugar into a sauté pan or deep frying pan. Add just enough water to cover and season with salt and pepper.

2. Bring to the boil and simmer, uncovered, for 10 minutes, shaking the pan occasionally, until the water has evaporated. The radishes will become a pinky-purple colour, and have a slight glaze.

3. Serve immediately, garnished with chervil or parsley.

BABY BEETS WITH FROMAGE FRAIS

SERVES 4

Steaming is a quick, but gentle method of cooking, retaining more of the vitamin C in vegetables than boiling. It's also a good way of reheating cooked foods, without destroying their shape and texture.

325 g (11 oz) cooked baby beetroot
125 ml (4 fl oz) fromage frais
1 tablespoon chopped dill
salt and pepper to taste
dill sprigs to garnish

1 Using a sharp knife, slice the beetroot at 2.5 cm (1 inch) intervals, leaving about 5 mm (¼ inch) intact at the base, to prevent them falling apart.

2 Place the beetroot in a heatproof dish which will fit inside a steaming basket or sieve, gently fanning them into position.

3 Place in the basket or sieve, cover and steam over boiling water for 8-10 minutes.

4 Mix the fromage frais with the chopped dill and seasoning.

5 Lift the beetroot out of the steamer and drain off any excess liquid. Arrange on a serving dish and spoon over the fromage frais. Serve immediately, garnished with dill.

PEAS WITH RADICCHIO

SERVES 4

Use frozen peas if fresh ones are not available. Young peas are the most successful – their sweetness complements the slightly bitter flavour of radicchio perfectly.

500 g (1 lb) shelled peas
mint sprig
salt and pepper to taste
25 g (1 oz) butter
125 g (4 oz) radicchio, finely shredded
mint sprigs to garnish

1 Put the peas in a saucepan containing about 1 cm (½ inch) depth of water. Add the mint and seasoning. Bring to the boil, cover and simmer gently for about 5 minutes, until the peas are tender.

2 Remove the mint and drain off the liquid from the peas. Add the butter and return to the heat. When the butter has melted, add the radicchio. Cook for a few seconds until the radicchio is warmed through, but retains its colour.

3 Serve immediately, garnished with mint.

INGREDIENTS

350g (12 oz/2½ cups) fresh
 raspberries
3 tablespoons orange juice
85-115g (3-4 oz/⅓-½ cup) caster
 sugar, depending on sweetness
preferred
150 ml (¼ pint/⅔ cup) low-fat
 natural yogurt
175g (6 oz/¾ cup) Greek yogurt
1 egg white
To decorate: fresh raspberries and
 lemon balm sprigs

METHOD   Preparation time: 15 minutes

Set freezer to rapid freeze. Purée the raspberries using a blender or food processor, then sieve into a large bowl to remove the seeds. Stir in the orange juice and 55g (2 oz/¼ cup) of the sugar. Mix together the two yogurts and stir into the fruit purée. Whisk lightly to mix.

Whisk the egg white until stiff then whisk in the remaining sugar. Fold into the fruit mixture. Pour into a rigid freezer-proof container, cover and freeze for about 2 hours, until slushy.

Remove the yogurt ice from the freezer and whisk until smooth. This will break down large ice crystals. Cover and return to the freezer for at least 4 hours until firm. Remember to return freezer to normal setting.
To serve, allow to soften in the fridge for 15 minutes before scooping into chilled dishes. Serve with extra fresh raspberries and lemon balm sprigs to decorate.

Serves 4

ICED EXOTIC FRUITS

INGREDIENTS

crushed ice
8 lychees
1 papaya
1 peach or nectarine
1 star fruit
1 pomegranate
225g (8 oz/1½ cups) strawberries,
* halved, or 150g (5 oz/1 cup)*
alpine strawberries
175g (6 oz/1¼ cups) raspberries
4-6 teaspoons orange flower water
To decorate: borage flowers
* (optional)*

METHOD

Preparation time: 15 minutes

Pile crushed ice on to four individual serving plates or one large platter. Put in the freezer until required. Peel the lychees and the papaya and remove the stones and seeds. Dice the papaya flesh.

Stone and slice the peach or nectarine. Thinly slice the star fruit. Quarter the pomegranate and carefully remove the seeds to a small bowl, catching any juice.

About ten minutes before serving, arrange all the fruits on the crushed ice and sprinkle with the pomegranate juice and orange flower water. Top with borage flowers for extra decoration, if liked. Place each serving on a second plate to serve.

NOTE:
Crush ice by wrapping in a clean tea towel and pounding with a rolling pin or mallet.

Serves 4

CHILLED FRUIT SOUP

INGREDIENTS

2 ripe Ogen or Galia melons
3 tablespoons caster sugar
1 large orange
225g (8 oz/1½ cups) small
  strawberries, halved
To decorate: borage flowers,
  (optional)

METHOD   Preparation time: 15 minutes

Halve the melons and discard the seeds. Scoop the flesh into a blender or food processor. Add the sugar and blend until smooth. Transfer to a bowl and chill for at least 1 hour or until almost ready to serve.

Using a sharp knife cut away the skin and pith of the orange. Holding over a bowl to catch the juice, cut out the orange segments. Cut these in half and add to the melon, along with any juice.

To serve, place four serving bowls on plates and surround with crushed ice. Spoon the soup into each and divide the strawberries between them. Decorate with borage flowers, if liked.

Serves 4

CHARENTAIS FRUIT CUPS

INGREDIENTS

175g (6 oz/1 cup) small strawberries
225g (8 oz/1½ cups) raspberries
2 tablespoons caster sugar
3-4 tablespoons Grand Marnier or
  Cointreau
2 charentais melons or other orange
  fleshed melons
To decorate: fruit leaves, if available

METHOD

Preparation time: 15 minutes

Hull the strawberries and halve them. Place in a bowl with the raspberries and sprinkle over the caster sugar and liqueur. Toss lightly to mix, cover and chill for at least 1 hour, or up to 3 hours. Put the melons to chill at the same time.

As soon as possible before serving cut the melons in half and remove a thin slice from the base of each half so they do not topple. Scoop out and discard the melon seeds.

Divide the fruit mixture between the melon halves and serve decorated with fruit leaves, if available.

NOTE:
It is important to choose melons that are ripe and fragrant for this simple refreshing dessert.

Serves 4

Irish Coffee Granita

INGREDIENTS

85g (3 oz/¹/₃ cup) soft brown sugar
600 ml (1 pint/2 cups) water
2 tablespoons instant coffee granules
6 tablespoons Irish whiskey
To decorate: 150 ml (¹/₄ pint/²/₃ cup)
  double (thick) cream (optional),
  cocoa powder

METHOD   Preparation time: 25 minutes

Set freezer to rapid freeze. Put the sugar and water in a medium saucepan and heat gently, stirring until the sugar is dissolved. Bring to the boil and allow to boil steadily for 5 minutes. Remove from the heat and stir in the instant coffee granules. Allow to cool.

When the coffee mixture is cold stir in the whiskey and transfer to a rigid freezer-proof container. Cover and freeze for about 2 hours until slushy. Remove the granita from the freezer and whisk to break up the ice crystals. Re-freeze as before. After 2 hours whisk again, cover and freeze until firm.

Ten minutes before serving, whip the cream, if using, until it forms soft peaks. Remove the granita from the freezer and allow to stand for 10 minutes at room temperature. Stir well until granular and spoon into tall stemmed serving glasses. If using, top each with a swirl of cream and dust lightly with cocoa powder. Remember to return freezer to normal setting.

Serves 4-6

LIGHT CHOCOLATE AND PEAR DESSERTS

INGREDIENTS

1 ripe pear
175g (6 oz/1¼ cup) raspberries
1 tablespoon caster sugar
1 x 225g (8 oz/1 cup) carton Greek yogurt
1 x 150 ml (5 fl oz/⅔ cup) carton natural yogurt
2 tablespoons cocoa powder, sifted
4 tablespoons icing sugar
To decorate: extra raspberries and mint sprigs

METHOD

Preparation time: 20 minutes

Peel and core the pear. Chop into small even pieces and place in a bowl with the raspberries. Sprinkle over the caster sugar and stir lightly to mix.

In a separate bowl whisk together the yogurts, cocoa powder and icing sugar until smooth. Spoon one third of the mixture into four individual serving glasses. Top this with half of the prepared fruit.

Continue layering the chocolate mixture and fruit, ending with a chocolate layer. Serve immediately, or lightly chilled, decorating each with extra raspberries and a mint sprig.

Serves 4

LIGHT MANGO CREAMS WITH PASSION FRUIT

INGREDIENTS

1 large ripe mango
3-4 tablespoons caster sugar
225 g (8 oz/1 cup) thick Greek
  yogurt
3 tablespoons orange juice
1 x 11g (½ oz/1 tablespoon) sachet
  powdered gelatine
1 egg white
4 passion fruit
To decorate: sprigs of mint or lemon
  balm

METHOD
Preparation time: 20–25 minutes

Lightly oil four individual pudding basins. Peel the mango and cut the flesh away from the stone. Chop roughly and place in a food processor or blender with 3 tablespoons caster sugar. Process until smooth. Transfer to a large bowl. Add the yogurt to the mango purée. Stir well and taste for sweetness, adding the extra tablespoon of sugar if preferred.

Put the orange juice in a small bowl or cup and sprinkle over the gelatine. Leave to soak for 1 minute then stand the bowl in a pan of hot water and stir until dissolved. Add to the yogurt mixture, stirring well. In a clean bowl, whisk the egg white until stiff. Using a large metal spoon, fold into the yogurt mixture. Spoon into the prepared pudding basins and chill for at least 1 hour until set.

To unmould the mango creams dip the moulds, one at a time, into warm water. Turn out on to individual serving plates. Cut the passion fruit in half and using a teaspoon scoop out the seeds and juice. Spoon over and around the mango creams. Decorate each with sprigs of mint or lemon balm.

Serves 4

MANDARIN AND GRAPE JELLY

INGREDIENTS

115g (4 oz/1 cup) seedless green or
    red grapes
2 x 11g (1 oz/2 tablespoons) sachet
    powdered gelatine
450 ml (¾ pint/1¾ cups) freshly
    squeezed mandarin juice
2-3 tablespoons sugar
To decorate: mandarin orange slices
    and mint sprigs or small vine leaves

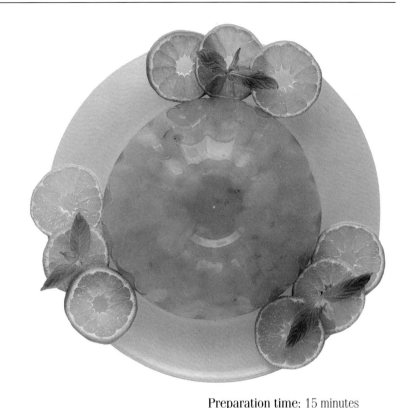

METHOD

Preparation time: 15 minutes

Halve the grapes and set aside. Pour
four tablespoons of cold water into a
small bowl and sprinkle the gelatine
over the surface. Leave for 2-3
minutes until spongy. Place the bowl
over a pan of hot water and stir until
completely dissolved.

Put the mandarin juice and sugar into
a saucepan with 300 ml (½ pint/1
cup) water. Bring to the boil, stirring
until the sugar is dissolved. Remove
from the heat and stir in the gelatine.
Strain into a jug and allow to cool
slightly.

Place the prepared grapes in a wetted
900 ml (1½ pint/2½ cups) mould.
Pour in the mandarin jelly liquid and
chill until set (about 2 hours). To
unmould, carefully dip the mould into
warm water and invert on to a
serving plate. Decorate with sliced
unpeeled mandarins and mint sprigs
or small vine leaves.

Serves 4

PAPAYA AND HONEY FROMAGE FRAIS

2 ripe papayas
1 tablespoon clear honey
225g (8 oz) fromage frais
8 ratafia or 4 amaretti biscuits
   (optional)
To decorate: mint sprigs

METHOD   Preparation time: 10 minutes
....

Halve the papayas and scoop out and discard the black seeds. Scoop the flesh from three of the halves into a food processor or blender, add the honey and blend until smooth. Transfer to a bowl.

Chop the flesh of the remaining papaya half. Stir the fromage frais into the fruit purée and then fold in the chopped fruit.

Spoon the mixture into four serving glasses and chill for at least 20 minutes before serving with ratafia or amaretti biscuits, if liked. Decorate with mint sprigs.

NOTE:
Try crumbling the amaretti biscuits in the base of the serving glasses before spooning in the fruit fromage frais.

Serves 4

BAKED APPLES WITH APRICOT AND COCONUT

INGREDIENTS

55g (2 oz) no soak dried apricots
25g (1 oz) sultanas or raisins
3 tablespoons dessicated coconut
3 tablespoons soft light brown sugar
½ teaspoon ground cinnamon
4 large cooking apples
*To serve: thick set yogurt or fromage
  frais*

METHOD

Preparation time: 15 minutes

Preheat the oven to 180° C/350° F/
Gas 4. Finely chop the apricots and
place in a bowl with the sultanas or
raisins, coconut, sugar and cinnamon.
Mix well.

Remove the cores from the apples.
Using a small sharp knife, make a
shallow cut around the middle of
each. Stand the apples in an
ovenproof dish.

Use the apricot mixture to fill the
apples, pressing in as firmly as
possible. Spoon four tablespoons
water around. Bake in the oven for
40-50 minutes until soft. Serve hot
with thick set yogurt or fromage frais.

Serves 4

INDEX